Praise for *Steeped in Stories:*
Timeless Children's Novels to Refresh Our Tired Souls

"Mitali Perkins's winsome way with words seeps through every page of this useful guide that's so much more than a guide. Her love of classic writing, even with all its flaws, serves as a compass for us to navigate the ins and outs of timeless stories so that they do more than entertain our modern craving for amusement."

—Tsh Oxenreider, author of *At Home in the World* and *Shadow and Light*

"Beautifully crafted, carefully researched, *Steeped in Stories* is a requisite immersion for all who enter the domain of children's literature."

—Rita Williams-García, *New York Times*–bestselling author and three-time National Book Award finalist

"*Steeped in Stories* is a timely exploration of timeless classics, clear-eyed about cultural blind spots, yet still enchanted by the wisdom, beauty, and wonder of these marvelous stories. This is one of the most brilliant guides to children's literature I've read."

—Karen Swallow Prior, professor and author of *On Reading Well: Finding the Good Life through Great Books*

"Stories have always been a place to escape when the world is overwhelming, and we need their refuge now more than ever. Mitali Perkins has given us such a gift in this collection."

—Jennifer Fulwiler, standup comic and bestselling author of *Your Blue Flame*

"Required reading for anyone who deigns to proffer an opinion on children's books written long ago."

—Betsy Bird, author, librarian, reviewer, and coauthor of *Wild Things: Acts of Mischief in Children's Literature*

"The best critics are those who inspire us to read more; Mitali Perkins has long been one of my favorite thinkers in the children's book world. *Steeped in Stories* is giving me to see how her deep faith informs her secular reading."

—Roger Sutton, editor in chief, *The Horn Book*

"Savor this feast of storytelling and be refreshed!"

—Mark Labberton, president of Fuller Theological Seminary

"Mitali Perkins is both a thoughtful storyteller and a wise guide who models how to mine for riches while recognizing the fool's gold in these beloved childhood classics."

—Sarah Arthur, author of *A Light So Lovely: The Spiritual Legacy of Madeleine L'Engle, author of* A Wrinkle in Time

"This book is a pure delight and a fierce testament to the power of stories to instruct and beguile. Perkins affectionately invites us to rediscover the virtues of the classics, while at the same time challenging us to think critically about their flaws."

—Léna Roy, director of teen programs at Writopia Lab and coauthor of *Becoming Madeleine: A Biography of the Author of* A Wrinkle in Time *by Her Granddaughters*

"*Steeped in Stories* beautifully uncovers for readers how healing and helpful reading children's classics can be at any age, stage, or season of life."

—Keri Wilt, writer, speaker, podcast host, and great-great-granddaughter of Frances Hodgson Burnett, the author of *The Secret Garden*

STEEPED IN STORIES

STEEPED IN STORIES

TIMELESS CHILDREN'S NOVELS TO REFRESH OUR TIRED SOULS

MITALI PERKINS

BROADLEAF BOOKS
MINNEAPOLIS

STEEPED IN STORIES
Timeless Children's Novels to Refresh Our Tired Souls

Cover design: Olga Grlic

Print ISBN: 978-1-5064-6910-2
eBook ISBN: 978-1-5064-6911-9

Printed in Canada

Contents

INTRODUCTION

THE TRANSFORMATIVE PRACTICE OF READING CHILDREN'S CLASSICS

My lifelong love of children's books begins on a humid summer's day in Flushing, Queens. Our family, newly immigrated from Kolkata, India, is unpacking suitcases in a small, stuffy apartment. I am seven years old, bored of settling in and grumpy.

Baba throws one of my older sisters a look, and Sonali reaches out a hand.

"Let's go," she says.

We walk ten blocks to a large, stately building. People are coming and going so freely that I wonder if they all live here. But after my sister signs us up at the front desk, she leads me into a room full of books, books, and more books.

"You can choose seven to take home and read," she tells me.

"For free?" I ask, wide-eyed.

"You have to return them," she says. "But then you get to pick seven more."

I rarely missed a weekly visit after that. The children's section of the Queens Public Library felt like Ali Baba's cave. Life grew more stressful—money was tight, our parents argued, my older sisters tested age-old boundaries that constrained the lives of "good Bengali girls"—but I had a safe retreat. Clutching a book, I slipped out of our bedroom window to the fire escape outside. Ahhh! The sounds, smells, and sights of the city street below me dissipated. I was no longer trapped in chronological time nor in geographical space. I was visiting Jo and her sisters in nineteenth-century Concord, Massachusetts, entering Narnia with Lucy and meeting Mr. Tumnus, sitting in Matthew's buggy as Anne made her way to Green Gables.

Perhaps you, too, remember the magic of vanishing into books as a child. You might have made your escape with a flashlight under the covers in bed or in another secret nook, but a book was your salve of choice. Back then, we consumed stories with both heart and mind engaged, fluidly crossing borders of culture and history. Immersing ourselves in many worlds, we grew in the skill of imagining other lives. In her now classic *Horn Book* essay "Against Borders," Hazel Rochman explains why stories have this mysterious power to build community: "They can break down borders. And the way that they do that is not with role models and recipes, not with noble messages about the human family, but with enthralling stories that make us imagine the lives of others. A good story lets you know people as individuals in all their particularity and conflict; and once you see someone as a person—their meanness and their courage—then you've reached beyond stereotype."

Out on that fire escape, I was hovering between two worlds—our apartment, which was basically still a Bengali village, and the overwhelming bustle and noise of New York City. Stories reduced the heat of life between cultures to a manageable simmer; it's likely they lowered the stress levels in your childhood as well. Don't you miss the peace that a good story left behind in your soul? Children's books can still do that good work for adults. "Think of children's books as literary vodka," author Katherine Rundell writes in *Why You Should Read Children's Books, Even Though You Are So Old and Wise*. She argues that children's fiction "helps us refind things we may not even know we have lost." Reading it as adults takes us back to a time when "new discoveries came daily and when the world was colossal, before the imagination was trimmed and neatened."

WHY DO GROWN-UPS STOP READING CHILDREN'S BOOKS?

Why, then, do most people stop reading children's books when they come of age? I've heard four main arguments, but none make sense.

First, some people look down on children's books as a lesser literary genre than books for adults. To me, the opposite often seems true. Some "grown-up" award-winning novels seem self-indulgent—written to display the author's intellectual prowess, mastery of language, and depth of thought. Children see right through that kind of pretension. They want the author to step aside and give the reader direct access. Storytellers in this genre have to create heroes' journeys with page-turning plots, characters who come alive, and a strong sense of place that transports readers into another reality. To do this, we must become ruthless eradicators of verbal fluff and restrainers of intellectual vanity.

Second, we might have stopped reading children's books because adults are embarrassed to be associated with children's activities. But there's no valid reason for shame. "There are good books which are only for adults, because their comprehension presupposes adult experiences, but there are no good books which are only for children," said W. H. Auden in an essay about Lewis Carroll. Cast aside fear and carry that children's book boldly with you on public transportation, in the café, or on holiday. "Is there any call for comment, if an adult reads them for himself?" asked J. R. R. Tolkien in a lecture. "Reads them as tales, that is, not studies them as curios. Adults are allowed to collect and study anything, even old theatre programmes or paper bags." C. S. Lewis, as was his wont, took on critics of children's literature head-on:

> Critics who treat "adult" as a term of approval, instead of as a merely descriptive term, cannot be adult themselves. To be concerned about being grown up, to admire the grown up because it is grown up, to blush at the suspicion of being childish; these things are the marks of childhood and adolescence. And in childhood and adolescence they are, in moderation, healthy symptoms. Young things ought to want to grow. But to carry on into middle life or even into early manhood this concern about being adult is a mark of really arrested development. When I was ten, I read fairy tales in secret and would have been ashamed if I had been found doing so. Now that I am fifty I read them openly. When I became a man I put away childish things, including the fear of childishness and the desire to be very grown up.

Third, we're told that children's books are moralistic, promoting a particular worldview and designed to inculcate virtues in the reader. Adult books are free from that kind of agenda, right? Not at all. Stories are by nature didactic. George Orwell was blunt about this in *Why I Write*: "No book is genuinely free from political bias. The opinion that art should have nothing to do with politics is itself a political attitude." D. H. Lawrence agreed, saying, "The essential function of art is moral . . . a morality which changes the blood, rather than the mind." All stories, not only the ones written for children, are transmitters of morality. Stories for children might be more powerful because a child has less capacity to discern and resist moral agendas, but the fact that they are aimed at children doesn't make them more didactic. And far from being simply "moral pap for the young," as Louisa May Alcott deprecatingly described her own stories, Rundell points out that children's books are actually *more* subversive because they are "written to be read by a section of society without political or economic power."

Fourth, grown-up literati are suspicious of stories with happy endings. Have you noticed that authors of fiction for adults seem abnormally fond of writing depressing endings? Many of today's award-winning novels for grown-ups should be labeled with a warning: *Not Suitable for an Upbeat Beach Holiday*. In contrast, good stories for children, after taking us through a hero's journey fraught with danger and loss, leave us with hope. Why is building hope considered less of a literary achievement than crushing it?

Now that I've (hopefully) convinced you to become a children's literature aficionado, let me disclose the truth: I write books for young readers. Consuming stories as a child brought me so much joy, perhaps it's not surprising that I ended up creating them. Much of my fiction illuminates growing up between cultures, like the novel *You Bring the Distant Near* and the picture book *Home Is in Between*, both of which are closest to a memoir of all my books. Others tackle injustice, like *Bamboo People*, a novel about refugees and child soldiers in Burma, or *Forward Me Back to You*, which delves into human trafficking and international adoption with—weirdly but appropriately if you know me—a Bollywood vibe, a touch of humor, and a bit of romance. I try my best to infuse my stories with hope. A good response from both adult and child readers is when something I write makes them laugh or cry—preferably both. But the best compliment is when someone of any age tells me they chose to reread one of my books.

REREAD CHILDREN'S CLASSICS IN HARD TIMES

"I'm not arguing that adults should only read children's fiction, but I'm arguing, very passionately, that adults who read children's fiction are offered something which perhaps other fiction cannot provide: a kind of hope and hunger," says Rundell. In her review of Rundell's essay, arts critic Jo

Hemmings sums up the gift that children's books bring to readers: "[Rundell's] argument is that sometimes adult literary fiction does not help. The old narratives, most commonly seen now in children's books, are the ones that best record human vice without despair. As she puts it, 'Children's fiction necessitates distillation: at its best, it renders in their purest, most archetypal forms hope, hunger, joy, fear.'"

In short, classics for young people are good stories, subversive and smart, unashamed to serve as vehicles to uplift and encourage. This makes them an excellent source of refreshment for tired souls. They are also likelier to be reread than any other kind of book. As C. S. Lewis wrote, "Where the children's story is simply the right form for what the author has to say, then of course readers who want to hear that will read the story or re-read it at any age."

Is there a book you first encountered as a child that you have reread time and again? If so, consider yourself blessed. "A classic is a book that has never finished saying what it has to say," says Italo Calvino in *The Uses of Literature*. Each time I reread a novel, the encounter is richer and deeper, perhaps because I myself am changed as a reader. Like aromatic leaves that eventually turn water into tea, so those stories changed me. But the process takes time. Madeleine L'Engle told a class of fourth graders in 1985, "The great thing about getting older is that you don't lose all the other ages you've been." When we reread a novel, we encounter it as all the ages we have been as well as the age we are now. Our souls are steeped in that story.

Rereading books also slows us down in the reception of a story, making room for the good work of loving transformation. "Love has its speed," writes theologian Kosuke Koyama in *Three Mile an Hour God*. "It is a different kind of speed from the technological speed to which we are accustomed. It goes on in the depth of life at three miles per hour. It is the speed we walk and therefore the speed the love of God walks." Because the last place my mind dwells before sleep is crucial, I try to replace a smartphone on my nightstand with a book I loved in childhood. Why not feed my unconscious soul with the goodness of a story instead of a depressing sweep through the headlines of the day? And if it's a reread, that's even better because the words and story are grooved more deeply into my memory.

"The Web provides a convenient and compelling supplement to personal memory," wrote Nicholas G. Carr in his prescient book *The Shallows: What the Internet Is Doing to Our Brains*. "But when we start using the Web as a substitute for personal memory, by bypassing the inner processes of consolidation, we risk emptying our minds of their riches." Like memorized poetry, children's stories that we know inside and out, even to the point of remembering passages by heart, may be mined as treasures by our sleeping brains. Rereading is deep, slow reading, and the practice is necessary to counterbalance the intake of information gained from a shallow, quick bounce around the internet.

Let me invite you, then, to make a cup of tea, grab that quilt your grandmother made, and join me in considering seven books that resonated profoundly in my childhood. I loved these books so much that I read them again at every stage of life (even sneaking off my college campus during final exams to find them in the public library). And now here I am, sitting down to write this book decades later. Here are the books we'll consider, in order of dates published. I've noted the places in which they were written to set them in their cultural and historical contexts.

- *Little Women* by Louisa May Alcott (1868–69, Concord, Massachusetts, United States)
- *Heidi* by Johanna Spyri (1880, Zurich, Switzerland)
- *A Little Princess* by Frances Hodgson Burnett (1887–88, serialized as "Sara Crewe, or What Happened at Miss Minchin's," Franklin Square, Washington, DC; 1905, revised, expanded, and published as *A Little Princess*, Great Maytham Hall, Kent, England)
- *Anne of Green Gables* by Lucy Maud Montgomery (1908, Cavendish, Prince Edward Island, Canada)
- *The Hobbit* by John Ronald Reuel Tolkien (1937, North Oxford, England, United Kingdom)
- *Emily of Deep Valley* by Maud Hart Lovelace (1950, Garden City, New York, United States)

- *The Silver Chair* by Clive Staples Lewis (1953, Headington Quarry, Oxford, England, United Kingdom)

You might keep turning the pages in *Steeped in Stories* without having read any of these children's novels, and that's fine. A warning, though—there are spoilers ahead. I invite you to go a bit deeper and let this book accompany a first reading of at least a few of the books, or maybe a reread of the ones you've already encountered. Most don't take long to finish. Those with expired copyrights are available online for free via the Gutenberg library (including *Little Women*, *Heidi*, *A Little Princess*, and *Anne of Green Gables*). And all have happy endings. At the end of each chapter, I've provided questions for reflection and discussion that you may either answer alone in a journal or use with a circle of friends. These questions are intended to slow us down and invite the story we have just considered to infuse our souls.

I'm hoping for several outcomes from our time together. First, we'll once again let ourselves fall openly and unashamedly in love with children's literature. Second, we'll discover (or rediscover) seven classics from former time periods that may help resist demoralizing patterns pressed upon us by our own era. Third, we'll be better equipped to engage critically with stories around issues like race, culture, and power. And fourth, thanks to a slow read of these seven novels, we'll be inspired to pursue virtue—specifically, the cardinal virtues of prudence, wisdom, justice, and temperance and the theological virtues of faith, hope, and love.

I owe a debt of gratitude to the authors of these seven novels. I see them as my spiritual and literary "aunties and uncles"—those who helped me navigate the stress of childhood. I like to imagine them as elderly relatives waiting on a front porch—or a fire escape—with an empty spot beside them, a place into which I sink and listen to their stories. To remind us of this role in my (and hopefully your) formation, I will use that honorific term from my culture when referring to the authors in each of their chapters: Aunt Louisa (as Louisa May Alcott's niece Lulu called her); Aunt Maud (the name Lucy Maud Montgomery preferred) and Auntie Maud (Maud Hart Lovelace); Uncle Jack (C. S. Lewis's lifelong nickname); Tante (*Aunt* in German, Johanna Spyri's mother tongue) Johanna; Uncle John Ronald (as Tolkien's nephew called him); and Aunt Frances (although she referred to herself as "Fluffina," I couldn't bring myself to do the same for Frances Hodgson Burnett).

But first, we have to address the elephant in the room (let's call him *Babar*). People of European descent wrote all seven books in bygone eras, which might be why many of their stories contain flaws related to race and culture. These are easier to spot from our vantage point in the present. Does this disqualify them from taking up space on our nightstands or bookshelves? Why spend time and money on books by dead white authors that promote racism or any other narrow-minded, power-based views of life?

REFLECT AND DISCUSS

1. The stories we love intersect the stories we live. Name a book that you loved in childhood. How did that story connect with your coming-of-age journey?
2. Which books, if any, did you read more than once as a child? Do you still reread them as an adult?
3. Have you read a new book written for young people recently? What did you enjoy about it and why?

1

DANGER AHEAD

THE ELEPHANT IN THE ROOM

As children, we read with fewer defenses and are wide open to the influence of stories. Years later, when we become adults, we find that the themes and messages in those narratives, for better or worse, are crafted deeply into the bedrock of our identities. Governments know that to fill children's stories with skewed views of certain groups of people is a powerful way to shape society. Many classic books for children, while not written primarily as propaganda, reflect colonial-era sensibilities about race, culture, and class. The debate over whether these books should be read by children in today's pluralistic, postmodern context is fierce and furious—and rightfully so, because stories received in childhood are powerful. How can we balance the reader's right to access literature from the past with our duty to protect and empower children, especially those from marginalized or oppressed communities?

SHOULD PROBLEMATIC CHILDREN'S BOOKS BE REMOVED FROM SHELVES?

Librarians, educators, and booksellers are grappling with this conundrum: How do we fight censorship and yet avoid damaging children's images of themselves and others by exposing them to racist and biased representations in books from the past? Take *Babar the Elephant* by Jean de Brunhoff, for instance, written in the 1930s. The book depicts an African elephant's return from France; he is fully clothed, "civilized," and walking on two feet to rule the naked four-footed beasts in his native land. Nicely reinforces colonialism, right? This book is being shifted from children's sections into adult sections of library shelves and bookstores throughout the world.

Tintin in the Congo by Belgian cartoonist Hergé is another book that comes under fire because of its view that the Congolese benefited from Belgian rule. (King Leopold II was actually one of the most ruthless colonial villains in history.) Tintin becomes a hero in the village, and a Congolese woman bows down to him, saying, "White man very great! Has good spirits. White mister is big juju man!" Responding to a complaint by a patron in October 2007, the Brooklyn Public Library in New York City placed the book in a locked back room, giving access only by appointment. The publisher also responded to concerns by placing a protective red band around the book with a warning about content and an introduction describing its historical context. As is typical, controversy increased interest in the book, and it rose to number eight on the Amazon best-seller list.

By now, you may be thinking of the Little House on the Prairie series, beloved by so many adult readers in the United States. Some want the book removed from libraries and schools for misrepresenting and even justifying the genocide of Native people living on this continent before European settlers arrived. I read the Little House series aloud to our sons when they were young—with parental input about the terrible history of people of European heritage commandeering land from Indigenous people. But what about children who encounter Ma's views of Indians and the book's skewed version of American history without informed adult guidance? Especially Native children? The debate over these books grew so intense that the Laura Ingalls Wilder Award for lifetime achievement in children's literature sponsored by the American Library Association was changed to the Children's Literature Legacy Award.

Even in more recent popular children's books, we find issues related to race and culture. For example, J. K. Rowling gives only the Black characters in her Harry Potter series a race attribution. Dean Thomas, "a black boy even taller than Ron," joins Harry at the Gryffindor table; Angelina Johnson is "a tall black girl who played Chaser on the Gryffindor Quidditch team"; Kingsley Shacklebolt is a "tall black wizard"; and Blaise Zabini is a "tall black boy with high cheekbones and long, slanting eyes." (Apparently, Black wizards are tall.) Rowling's Asian characters are given an ethnic identity by their names—Cho Chang (an odd combination of a Korean surname and a Chinese surname) and the Patil sisters, for example. But with only nonwhite races explicitly mentioned, it's likely that for readers and for the writer herself, all other characters default to white—especially with nonverbal descriptions like "blushing" and "growing pale."

Many of the seven authors we are about to read are outdated or worse when it comes to a portrayal of race and culture. In Narnia, dark-skinned Calormenes are a cruel enemy; in Middle Earth, swarthy, slant-eyed beings are not to be trusted. L. M. Montgomery talks about "jewing down" a price and presents a negative view of French-speaking Canadians. Servants like Asia and Silas in L. M. Alcott's books are presumably Black and serve as foils with no backstory. One of the boys in Emily's wrestling club uses an ethnic slur about Syrians in *Emily of Deep Valley*, and the Indian sailor in Frances Hodgson Burnett's *Little Princess* is an exoticized, mystical other.

That's a lot to process, isn't it? We'll take a closer look at these issues in each novel. For a few books aimed at younger readers, including *A Little Princess*, *Anne of Green Gables*, and *Emily of Deep Valley*, I provide a sample of possible conversations while reading these books with children in your life. I hope these serve as helpful prompts for dialogue. Some would argue that we shouldn't read them at all in our era; I disagree, and I'll try to show you why.

As I've tuned into the debate over books from the past, I've noticed that protests try to limit the circulation of only a few classics with issues, while other problematic books continue to reach children without any objection. For example, Hugh Lofting's *The Story of Doctor Dolittle*, a Newbery Medal–winning novel written in 1920, keeps getting a new lease on life thanks to movie adaptations. This is despite the fact that the book devotes several chapters to Prince Bumpo's longing to be white-skinned. I'm still trying to understand why some books escape our ire while others stoke it. If we remove a few books from circulation because of race, culture, or colonialism, why not all of them?

When we consider books written in the past and include filters for narrow or damaging views of gender, ability, and class, the list of books deemed problematic grows even longer. If our generation of gatekeepers sets up criteria to assess classics for current circulation, we might end up pulling almost all of them. I've visited countries where governments have done that; eradicating the record of a cruel past doesn't lead to human flourishing.

There has to be a better way.

COULD WE EDIT THEM?

Sometimes a few words or phrases are *bowdlerized* in the attempt to make a book more palatable to present generations. In 1818, Thomas Bowdler published his *Family Shakspeare* [*sic*] promising that "those words and expressions are omitted which cannot with propriety be read aloud in a family." The sanitized volume was popular in his Victorian era; within eleven years of his death in 1825, the word *bowdlerize* had been coined and referred to expurgating books or other texts of terminology and content deemed improper or offensive. Today, for example, we have a bowdlerized version of *Huck Finn* by Mark Twain, which replaces the more than two hundred occurrences of the n-word with the word *slave*.

Even though it's a way to compromise and keep a book on the shelves, not many of us seem to like bowdlerization as a solution. Some object to it on the grounds that changing a few words can't take racism out of the core structure of a book. They still want that story completely *removed* from any collection read by today's children. Their opponents agree with them when it comes to not changing a word in the book—but only because they want the classics to *stay* in any such canon. Others believe the book should remain on the shelves *with restrictions on access* so that teachers and librarians may use them to instruct the next generation about history that shouldn't be repeated. This latter strategy only works if most or all adult educators are motivated and equipped to teach critically—two prerequisites questioned by people championing children in marginalized communities.

Then there's the argument that we can't wordsmith or edit a book because it overrides authorial intent. In this view, bowdlerization can't be accomplished by anyone other than the author. In 1952, for example, Laura Ingalls Wilder changed a word in her book after a reader wrote to her about a particular line: "There were no people there. Only Indians." Weren't Indians people, the reader asked? Ursula Nordstrom, Wilder's editor at Harper & Row, forwarded the letter's feedback to the author, who changed the word *people* to *settlers*: "There were no settlers there. Only Indians." Wilder was still alive when she authorized the change. But did her edit address the problems buried deeply throughout the entire story? And who has the right to bowdlerize a book once the author is dead?

I bowdlerized one of my own books. When *The Sunita Experiment*, my debut novel, was released in 1993 from Little,

Brown, a reviewer chastised me for the "unnecessary exoticization" of my protagonist. Here's the original ending:

> Michael is waiting for her. Slowly, she glides down, her golden bangles clinking together in melodious, graceful accompaniment.
>
> "You look . . . just like I thought you would, Sunni," he whispers when she reaches him. "Are you sure you're still Sunita Sen and not some exotic Indian princess coming to cast a spell on me?"
>
> "I'm sure, Michael," she tells him, giving him one of her trademark smiles just to prove it.

I fumed at first, but dang it, she was right. I had grown up resisting the fetishizing of Asian women by some men. *Exotic Indian princess?* What was I thinking? Enduring the twinge of shame, I moved on and tried to learn from my mistake. In 2005, when Little, Brown decided to reissue the book, they asked if I wanted to make any changes. "Yes!" I shouted, pumping my fist. Here's how the book ends now:

> Michael is waiting for her. Slowly, she glides down, her golden bangles clinking together in melodious, graceful accompaniment.
>
> "You look . . . just like I thought you would, Sunni," he whispers when she reaches him. "Are you sure you're still the same Sunita Sen? The California girl?"

"I'm sure, Michael," she tells him, giving him one of her trademark smiles just to prove it.

What a relief, right? A problem, however, in fixing errors in my work is that I won't be around forever. If there's an outcry over another flaw or "ism" in one of my novels one day, who would be handed the baton to bowdlerize? My editors? They may be dead too. Our sons would turn down the job. Any grandchildren (assuming I have some) will likely do the same. Even if pressured into changing my work, how can they be sure they aren't accidentally introducing problematic mores of their era into the story? Next in line to fix mistakes: a bewildered great-grandchild.

MY ANSWER . . . LET MANY STORIES COME

So what do we do if we care about both combating censorship *and* protecting children from damaging representation or deceitful versions of history in books from the past? My own answer, as often happens, is to respond with a question. What to do with problematic books for children written in the *present*?

Despite my best attempts to infuse my books with truth, justice, humility, and love, they are likely laden with "isms" I can't see because I'm limited by a particular cultural and historical context. Librarians in future generations might toss them into a recycling bin. (They might be doing that now, for all I know. If they are, please don't tell me.) I'm certain that some books written by a diversity of authors today will join the ranks of classics to be reread into the future. But there's no doubt that newer books are flawed too, with problems particular to here and now that are difficult for us to perceive. Both we who are creators of stories and we who are readers are immersed in this moment. It will be the job of literary gatekeepers in years to come to debate the drawbacks and merits of books published today.

The fact that all stories are imperfect means we must equip young people to read critically. In the midst of the fiery debate, I propose that adults who are committed to educating this generation—parents, grandparents, teachers, librarians, writers, and others—find common ground by agreeing on one key premise: crossing as many borders as possible in childhood, which includes engaging with a wide range of people *and* stories, is vital in developing discernment.

The novelist Chimamanda Adichie presented "The Danger of a Single Story" in her now classic 2009 TED talk, in which she argues that inherent in the power of stories is the danger of knowing only one story about a group. "The single story creates stereotypes, and the problem with stereotypes is not that they are untrue but that they are incomplete," she said. "They make one story become the only story." To counter this, Adichie advocated the creation and consumption of *many* stories about people and cultures.

I believe this "many story strategy" can also mediate a single story from the past, even an outdated book that condones, outright or subconsciously, the supremacy of one race over another. To dilute the toxicity of an "ism" that creeps into any book, past, present, or future, the best-case scenario is that we provide children with a *multitude* of stories told by a *wide* range of voices.

Reading many stories as a child builds a capacity to see underlying messages about the "other" as well as to imagine other lives. Take me, for example. As I devoured a wide variety of stories, I gained an ease at stepping into any hero's shoes regardless of identity. If a Korean boy only reads about Korean boys in childhood, for example, his imagination remains somewhat stunted; he will have to work hard to develop a fluency in crossing borders because he didn't practice that skill in childhood. It will take effort to see himself as a hero who is a Middle Eastern woman. Meanwhile, I can proficiently identify with almost any protagonist because I had to do that as a child in every story I read.

BOOKS AS MIRRORS FOR THE MARGINALIZED

I am grateful for a flexible imagination formed by reading about people in eras and demographic categories different from mine. Yet it *is* profoundly moving to see my ethnicity reflected in a protagonist in a book I'm reading, since that experience was so rare during my childhood. When I wandered the library shelves as a feral reader decades ago, books written by brown and Black authors were few and far between. The world of children's literature in the United States of my youth was decidedly not multicultural— and sadly, I didn't discover rare finds that *were* available when I was a child, like Mildred Taylor's *Roll of Thunder, Hear My Cry* or *Gay Neck: The Story of a Pigeon* by the Bengali writer Dhan Gopal Mukerji, which won the Newbery Medal in 1927. Today, the compendium of children's literature is widening slowly, thanks to an excruciating effort to transform the publishing industry. A plethora of stories featuring many kinds of heroes is a gift to the world's children, especially those who now see their identities mirrored by the protagonists of their favorite books.

Both are needed: stories as mirrors of some of our identities and stories as windows into unfamiliar ones, a metaphor coined by Dr. Rudine Sims Bishop. But a story, by nature, is an invitation to become skilled in crossing borders via the imagination. In a literate utopia, empowered children will read freely and widely, consuming stories from the past and in the present. They will develop the capacity to see mores and agendas and begin discerning an answer to that essentially human question, *What is good?*

We're not living in an ideal world yet, and at times our present situation feels more like a dystopia than the opposite. But could we, as adults who love children's literature and children, agree to provide them with many stories that reflect a multitude of identities?

A FUTURE ABUNDANCE OF STORIES

For now, with shrinking budgets for public and school libraries, a many-story strategy might not be possible, especially for families with limited resources like my own when I was a child. I put the challenge to those who value the deepening and widening of children's literature—whether we act as citizens, consumers, creators, or some combination of the three.

As citizens, we fight to keep a wide selection of books available in public and school libraries with our votes, tax dollars, and advocacy. Libraries matter to marginalized children because that's likely where they will find a variety of stories that open windows into other lives—both from the past and in the present—as well as provide mirrors of their identities.

As consumers, we purchase books to send a message to publishers about the sort of stories we want them to provide in the market. In the face of our communal need to heal from a history of genocide, colonialism, slavery, and other atrocities, we support excellent new books written by descendants of suffering people.

And as creators, our call is to write a fresh selection of engaging and inspiring stories for the next generation. This will require excellence and courage. In the tenth chapter of this book, I provide guidelines for those eager to respond to this challenge.

In the face of fiery arguments over censorship and justice, which I'm certain will continue, let's keep dreaming of a world full of astute young readers encountering a wide variety of many stories. The mystery of a beloved story is that it intersects with the reader's particular hero's journey, so we can empower young people to forage freely and find their own favorites. The more stories they choose, the less a single one commandeers the power to form their souls.

In that golden era, we'll have taught children to think critically about books, both in the present and in the past, by educating ourselves and modeling a breadth and depth of story consumption. Thanks to advocacy, consumption, and creativity, new books will be penned by a diversity of authors and read widely. Those stories will decolonize our imaginations and become classics that stay in print and on libraries' shelves.

Won't you join me in making that vision a reality?

"I'm in," you say as you refill your cup. "But in the meantime, should we as grown-ups keep rereading the problematic classics we loved in childhood? I certainly don't want to endorse racism or colonialism."

Here's my answer to that question: "Yes! Indeed, we *must*!" We're about to take a closer look at why and how children's stories from the past can revitalize older souls, especially in a demoralized era. After you ponder the questions at the end of this chapter, get a scone and some clotted cream and meet me in the next one.

REFLECT AND DISCUSS

1. Describe a book you read in childhood that required you to cross a border of race, culture, and power to imagine another life.

2. Describe a book you read recently that required you to cross a border of race, culture, and power to imagine another life. (If you can't think of any, ask a trusted curator in person or online to recommend a title. Read it and reflect on how it changed or moved you.)

3. If the children in your care are voracious readers and find their way to books on their own, do you monitor their choices? Why or why not?

4. Would you read the Babar, Tintin, or Little House books aloud to children? If so, how would you moderate the discussion, if at all?

5. Would your reading of those books differ depending on which children are in the listening circle around you?

6. Do you think a book should ever be bowdlerized— that is, have offensive language or content removed or changed?

7. Are you comfortable seeing books for young readers with "questionable content" marked by booksellers or librarians with paper bands, placement on separate shelving, or other indicators? Why or why not?

2

SEVEN BOOKS, SEVEN VIRTUES

FINDING GOODNESS IN PERSON

W hy should adults keep reading children's books from the past? I'll give you two reasons. The first, as we considered in the previous chapter, is to develop the critical thinking necessary to shepherd the next generation. This takes work, which we will do together as we delve into the seven novels in this book and discuss some of their flaws. And then, in the last chapter, I'll review and summarize questions related to race, culture, and power to ask of all stories, whether written in the past or in the present. I want to become the kind of reader who can help young people discern and, if needed, resist subversive messages.

The second reason to revisit books from the past as adults is to move forward with humility in our own formation. Adults are less susceptible than children to fiction's subversive power of building a subterranean morality. Still, good children's stories from the past can refresh and shape our tired souls, especially when we are hobbled by our divisive and despondent age. As we discussed earlier, they can be much better than adult literature at generating hope.

But first, we must try to define the word *good*. Is virtue bound to a particular culture or era? Can we all agree on what is good—or is consensus on goodness simply impossible?

THREE MODERNITIES: CHECKS AND BALANCES

Premodern (think: village) cultures, which include European cultures in the Middle Ages as well as contemporary groups in different parts of the world, each have their own beliefs about goodness and evil. A modern definition of *good* arose in Europe in the sixteenth and seventeenth centuries and was based on both Judeo-Christian doctrine and the humanistic values that emerged after the Renaissance during the Enlightenment. Some believe the era of modernity ended by 1930, others after World War II in 1945, but most agree that it was gone by the late twentieth century. That's when the Western world moved into postmodernity, as more and more people found it difficult to accept a shared, absolute definition of morality.

As a brown person born in a once-colonized country, I have wondered if books by writers of European descent imposed modernity over my Bengali family's premodernity. Were my favorite childhood books yet another weapon in the colonizing arsenal? Is that why I felt—and feel—so at home when I read them? But deeper reflection reveals that I was formed by three value systems: the premodernity of my parents' Bengali village, the modernity of my Western education and cultural milieu in which I lived during childhood and young adulthood, and the postmodernity of today's context. These pushed against each other in my psyche as I sought to define goodness.

Classic novels definitely exposed me to modern values and even prepared me to claim some as my own. But as I've given my love for them a closer look, I can see that my premodern Bengali village heritage played a large part in why I made myself at home in these books. My parents taught me to savor the beauty of the natural world through Bengali poetry and songs, for example. The North American pop songs playing on the radio during my childhood ignored that beauty, but I found a celebration of it in old-fashioned books. Those same songs glorified romance even as many of my classmates' parents who had "fallen in love" were divorcing. Meanwhile, my own parents, who met each other for the first time on the day of their wedding, stayed together through ups and downs. I saw their marital duty and fidelity reflected in vintage children's books. Ma and Baba also passed on a Bengali freedom of emotion—license to weep, rage, and laugh—and an honoring of elders. These values seemed the exception rather than the rule in North American culture but turned up frequently in stories from the past. My two older sisters took care of me, and I looked up to them; this sibling bond was mirrored more by the classic fiction I was reading than by the squabbling and eye-rolling among brothers and sisters in our suburban neighborhood.

As I grew older, my ancestors' premodernity continued to push against and restrict the influence of modernity in my formation. Even with a top-notch college education that challenged me to be a critical thinker, I might still have internalized white-centeredness were it not for the robust pride my parents passed on in our heritage. Bengalis, in fact, can be *too* proud of that identity. Some of my relatives divided the world into two groups: Bengali (superior) and non-Bengali (including other Indians, whites, other Asians, other races—sadly ranked in that order, from less to more inferior). *Why would anyone want to be anything but Bengali?* was the implicit message, for better or worse. In turn, postmodern thinking helped me reject preferences for light skin over dark and for sons over daughters that were also a part of my culture of origin and in some modern literature.

Premodernity resisted modernity, postmodernity pushed back against premodernity, and so on. As champion of temperance Louisa May Alcott might notice benevolently, the eras moderated each other in my formation.

The college students and writers I sometimes teach who were formed in postmodernity tend to appreciate and sometimes even revere my proximity to premodern Bengali village language and culture—that is, until they learn that my great-grandmother was married off at age nine to a husband more than double her age and that this practice was accepted and common. This chunk of ancestral history—even in their "all cultures have equal value" framework—elicits expressions of disgust. Resistance to a child getting married comes from a deeply held value of defining an "age of consent." But where does that value come from? *Why* should children be protected from slavery, trafficking, forced labor, pornography, body mutilation, or child marriage?

When I pose this question in the classroom, answers typically circle around the fact that children can't protect themselves. The strong must protect the weak. This is just. Merciful. Even good. I press on: How do we define *good?* My ancestral culture once believed child marriage was good. The custom protected a girl, they believed, allowing her to be known and loved as a child in a household economy where she would eventually gain matriarchal power. The students shrug, mulling that over and trying to lean into a deeply held value of tolerance that could help them accept this practice. Still, they hate the thought of a girl getting married at age nine.

Cultural and historical contexts matter. The problem is that when you're steeped in them, they shape you—for better and worse—and it's hard to see how. So what is "goodness," and who gets to determine its shape and scope? No single culture or era can fully hold the answer to that question; cultures and eras, like individuals, are marred and beautiful at the same time. To widen the narrow vision of our own perspectives, I encourage readers to cross borders of race and culture and learn from a diversity of contemporary storytellers. But to widen the narrow, limited vision of our own era, we may—dare I say, must—also cross borders into the past to seek goodness in stories there as well. As the *Atlantic Monthly* editors posited in publishing poems written by dead people, "Sometimes we need to turn to the past to help make sense of the present."

When we open ourselves to writing from the past, we resist the danger of "presentism," a concept Alan Jacobs discusses in *Breaking Bread with the Dead: A Reader's Guide to a More Tranquil Mind*. The title of Jacobs's book is based on a quote from the poet W. H. Auden, who once said that "art is our chief means of breaking bread with the dead." Auden believed that "without communion with the dead, a fully human life is impossible."

A fully human life is the good life we desire. Inevitably, when I talk about cultural pluralism and our human quest to define goodness, one of my students will approach me one-on-one and ask a marvelous question: "How do *you* define good, Ms. Perkins?" Apparently, they aren't the only ones who want to know. If you type my name in any online browser search bar (as we authors tend to do), a common phrase that pops up in the suggestions is "Mitali Perkins beliefs." I can't write a book like this without making those clear.

FINDING GOODNESS IN PERSON

What is good? I would like to hear your answer if you have one; please tell me face-to-face if we ever have the pleasure of meeting in person. Here's mine. When I asked that question on a spiritual search that began in childhood, it led me to another question: *Who* is good?

After some study of comparative religions and philosophies, I began to see that the goodness I sought was personified by one Jewish man. I discovered him in a sacred book I used to think was only for Westerners. This swarthy (as I imagined him) storyteller was a postmodern champion of the marginalized, a hater of injustice, a tolerant friend to diverse people. In his words and life, I recognized virtues I cherished in my beloved collection of "modern" children's books as well as values of Middle Eastern origin that were prized in my family's premodernity, like hospitality, humility, and honor. Best of all, this person didn't just teach about and model goodness; according to writers of the Bible's New Testament, he died and then defeated death to make a way for us to gain goodness.

Without having entered any North American church (apart from a visit to a Christmas service held in the chapel at the college where I was studying), at age nineteen I privately decided to "take Jesus as my guru." My baptism in a fountain on campus during the busy noon hour made the affiliation public, and I've followed Jishu or Isa (as Bengalis call Jesus—the former term used by Hindus, the latter by Muslims) ever since. This led me to join a global church of Jesus-followers, first established by my "guru" in Jerusalem, that is now increasingly made up of people of non-Western origin. The majority of music, liturgy, teaching, and prayers expressed in that church has shifted from English to languages spoken in Africa, Asia, and Latin America.

While most of today's thriving churches are no longer in places like Rome or London, history matters in religion as well as in the wider culture. That's why I've drawn upon ancient church tradition as the source of the seven virtues explored in seven children's novels. When it comes to good character, these aren't an exhaustive list of attributes, but they do provide us with a start. The four cardinal virtues—justice, temperance, prudence, and courage—originated in Greek thought and were co-opted by early leaders of the church, who added the three theological virtues—faith, hope, and charity (love)—that are named in 1 Corinthians 13. Each novel illuminates one of these seven virtues.

These timeless children's stories also shed light on seven fiery vices inside our souls that are stoked by heat from our culture and era: rigidity, alienation, despair, pusillanimity, self-indulgence, favoritism, and rashness. Each virtue battles a particular vice, with love extinguishing rigidity; faith, alienation; hope, despair; courage, pusillanimity; temperance, self-indulgence; justice, favoritism; and prudence, rashness. This list of vices, like the virtues, is not comprehensive. Sadly, humanity is creative in finding new ways to do evil.

CAN ANY OR ALL HUMANS BE GOOD?

As the novelist Aleksandr Solzhenitsyn wrote, "The line separating good and evil passes . . . right through every human heart—and through all human hearts. This line shifts. Inside us, it oscillates with the years. And even within hearts overwhelmed by evil, one small bridgehead of good is retained. And even in the best of all hearts, there remains . . . a small corner of evil." Through the centuries, various branches of the church have debated whether any virtues can be realized through the efforts of human souls, which are inevitably tainted by vice.

Because of this malady, some believe that only God may be truly virtuous and that it's useless for humans to try. Others disagree, arguing that human effort in practicing virtue is a vital part of God's care for the world. The *Catechism of the Catholic Church*, for example, describes a mysterious partnership between God and humanity:

> Human virtues acquired by education, by deliberate acts and by a perseverance ever-renewed in repeated efforts are purified and elevated by divine grace. With God's help, they forge character and give facility in the practice of the good. The virtuous man is happy to practice them.
>
> It is not easy for man, wounded by sin, to maintain moral balance. Christ's gift of salvation offers us the grace necessary to persevere in the pursuit of the virtues. Everyone should always ask for this grace of light and strength, frequent the sacraments, cooperate with the Holy Spirit, and follow his calls to love what is good and shun evil.

By this definition, which requires a partnership with the divine, can people outside the church be virtuous? Again, there is debate, but to me, the naysayers' arguments ring falsely. My answer to this question is a resounding yes. It derives from my understanding of theology and from what I have seen in my relatives, friends, and students: people in other faith traditions and people without any faith in God may indeed be virtuous. Human beings are the *imago*

Dei—created in God's image—and designed to practice and yearn for justice, temperance, courage, prudence, faith, hope, and love.

As Saint Paul encouraged his friends in Philippi, "Whatever is true, whatever is noble, whatever is right, whatever is pure, whatever is lovely, whatever is admirable—if anything is excellent or praiseworthy—think about such things" (Philippians 4:8). Excellent and praiseworthy behavior and practices are seen in every culture: in art and music created by people outside the Christian faith and in actions and deeds of people who have neither entered a church nor read a Bible. For an exposition of this thesis, I recommend reading Madeleine L'Engle's *Walking on Water: Reflections on Faith and Art*, in which she discusses how atheists can create art that is more beautiful and true than art by less-talented artists of deep faith. That's why, for the purposes of this book, we will talk about the virtues as habits that lead to a good life for people both inside and outside the church.

A TUTOR OF VIRTUE AND VICE

That being said, when anyone wants to see a portrait of this life, I suggest reading Matthew, Mark, Luke, and John, the writers of four short narratives called the "Gospels" in the New Testament. They featured such a just, temperate, courageous, prudent, hopeful, faithful, and loving life in a person from Nazareth named Jesus. All four authors claimed that he was killed on a cross, defeated death by returning to life, and departed historical time. Before he left, he promised to send a holy helper to his disciples, the "Spirit of God." His friends had no idea what he was saying at the time, but the book of Acts in the Bible's New Testament describes what happened when this unseen companion arrived. An uneducated, powerless band of fearful, hopeless, faithless friends of Jesus became the "body of Christ" and began to change the world.

Since I joined the church through baptism, I, too, have experienced the presence and power of God's Spirit in encouraging virtue and avoiding vice. This "tutor" has prompted me to confess pusillanimity, self-indulgence, favoritism, and foolishness; offered grace after failures in courage, temperance, justice, and prudence; and filled up low reservoirs of faith, hope, and love. Such mysterious, invisible help from God is so vital in my journey that I must make that provision clear, especially in a book I'm writing to explore the virtuous life.

In the Hebrew Scriptures, years before Jesus walked the earth, the prophet Micah wrote, "He has told you, O mortal, what is good; and what does the Lord require of you but to do justice, and to love kindness, and to walk humbly with your God" (Micah 6:8 NRSV). Despite their flaws and errors, the seven children's novels we are about to explore inspired me as a child to do justice, love mercy, and walk humbly with

God. My tutor still puts them to use in my formation as I reread them every year. I hope you too receive encouragement and refreshment as you join me.

We begin with an exploration of the virtue of love and the vice of rigidity in *Anne of Green Gables* by Lucy Maud Montgomery, a novel written more than a century ago but still read widely today.

REFLECT AND DISCUSS

1. What is "good"? Compose a brief definition.
2. Who is "good"? Name and describe one of your heroes of virtue.
3. Did any value systems, cultures, or modernities compete with each other in your formation during childhood?
4. Go on a hunt for "good" behavior this week. Write down at least two examples of excellent or praiseworthy deeds that illustrate a particular virtue in action.
5. Write a brief definition of each of the seven virtues: faith, hope, love, prudence, courage, justice, and temperance. Try to use seven words or less for each definition.
6. Which two virtues do you most want to nurture in yourself? Why?

3

RIGIDITY AND LOVE

ANNE OF GREEN GABLES BY L. M. MONTGOMERY

It won't make a bit of difference where I go or how much
I change outwardly; at heart I shall always be your little
Anne, who will love you and Matthew and dear Green
Gables more and better every day of her life.

—Anne Shirley

When I first encountered Anne Shirley, I was eleven
years old, and my family was living as expatriates
in Mexico City. Baba was working long hours as a harbor
engineer and longing to rest on the weekends, but he devoted

his Saturdays to taking me to an English-language children's library across town. That's where I first met Lucy Maud Montgomery, and within a year, I had devoured all twenty of her novels.

I felt immediately at home with the invitation from Aunt Maud (the name she preferred over Lucy) to delight in natural beauty. Baba also shared his gift of wonderment with us. He taught us to pay attention to the symmetry of a butterfly, the majesty of a mountain, the play of clouds across a windy sky. "What a Creator!" he'd whisper, and we'd keep still until a hummingbird left the bottlebrush bush. Years later, when our father's bones and brain were shrinking, a lifelong practice of taking delight in nature sustained him. We wheeled him out to the garden, where he'd count petals, his fingers gentle as they slowly spun each flower. Maybe that's why Anne's starry-eyed rapture over beauty in the natural world seemed familiar to me; it was what I always saw in Baba's eyes.

This Canadian redhead, adopted by an elderly couple living on Prince Edward Island (PEI), has become a dearly beloved character throughout the world. Fans of Aunt Maud's novel respond to Anne's expressiveness, imagination, and capacity for delight. A multitude of Japanese tourists have made a pilgrimage to PEI because the book is so popular in their country. In an interview with Dr. Yukari Yoshihara, a literature teacher at the University of Tsukuba,

BBC journalist Robin Levinson-King noted that "Anne is popular with Japanese women especially, Ms Yoshihara says, because the world of Green Gables is filled with 'kawaii,' which means the quality of being cute, romantic and beautiful in Japanese."

Professor Yoshihara also sees the book as subversive in Japan when it comes to gender. That was especially true in 1952, when Hanako Muraoka first translated it into Japanese. Terry Dawes, a lifelong PEI resident, filmed a 2014 documentary on Japan's love for Anne and interviewed dozens of fans of the book. "Anne Shirley provides a way of acting out, to a point, without ever transgressing fully," he told Levinson-King. "Ultimately, she does the right thing by her family, her adopted family." Chinese readers love Anne too, and I've known many readers of Indian origin (like me) who are drawn to the novel's intersection of gender equality and familial duty.

Then there are the particular ways each of us identifies with her. My connection centers on Anne's love of nature and her outsider's view of religion. Aunt Maud was married to a Presbyterian pastor for years. Maybe that's why, when I reread the novel as the spouse of a Presbyterian pastor myself, I noticed its snarky view of church. When we first meet her, Anne is "next door to a perfect heathen," in the words of Marilla Cuthbert, an older woman who lives in a house called Green Gables. In Anne's childlike, candid opinion, the sermon is long and boring and the minister clearly doesn't have enough imagination. But that's not all; an elder named Mr. Bell prays for far too long and seems bored with his own prayer. "I think he thought God was too far off to make it worth while," Anne says. The audacity of a pastor's wife writing such descriptions of church! What a fantastic use of fiction, right?

I also respond to the insightful teaching about prayer laced throughout the story. Marilla is reluctant to teach Anne the "childish classic, 'Now I lay me down to sleep'" because it seems "entirely unsuited to this freckled witch of a girl who knew and cared nothing about God's love, since she had never had it translated to her through the medium of human love." When Anne is at church for the first time, Aunt Maud gives an example of simple, authentic prayer. Sitting in the pew while Mr. Bell drones on, Anne glimpses the beauty of the birches, lake, and sunshine and thanks God for them from her heart. A bit later in the book, Anne reflects profoundly that "saying one's prayers isn't exactly the same thing as praying."

As a child reader, I knew nothing about church or Jesus. The first time I heard about Jesus's love for children, I responded much as Anne did to a vivid chromolithograph in the sitting room of Green Gables called "Christ Blessing Little Children." She notices a small, shy girl in a blue dress who "crept shyly up on the outside of the crowd, hoping nobody would notice her—except Him." Aunt Maud helps us see Jesus's response to the outsider through Anne's eyes: "It's likely He did, don't you think? I've been trying to imagine it all out—her edging a little nearer all the time until she was quite close to Him; and then he would look at her and put His hand on her hair and oh, such a thrill of joy as would run over her!" I'm so grateful it ran over me.

But before we soak in the love Aunt Maud offers so generously in *Anne of Green Gables*, let's look at how her context shaped her to write about the "other."

ACADIANS, JEWISH PEOPLE, AND ADOPTEES AS OUTSIDERS

Here's an important question to help us become more astute at critiquing xenophobia in a novel: Is a negative view of the stranger embedded in the "bones of the book," stemming from the author's own belief, or is it expressed by a flawed character in the story? If the latter, readers learn to resist the prejudiced secondary character's viewpoint, and the wider novel can espouse the truth that outsiders should be welcomed. If the former—if the bias comes from the omniscient narrator or exemplary character—well, the message is more insidious. In Aunt Maud's case, at least from my perspective, it's a mix of both.

The author slyly and adeptly critiques the fear of the foreigner by filling Anne's story with the perspectives of narrowminded women like Rachel Lynde and Marilla Cuthbert.

Mrs. Lynde, for example, jokes about Irish people by saying, "A body can get used to anything, even being hanged, as the Irishman said." In my view, a story isn't toxic when a biased character makes a biased comment. When Anne buys dye for her hair from a Jewish peddler, her response in contrast to Marilla's is telling:

> "Anne Shirley, how often have I told you never to let one of those Italians in the house! I don't believe in encouraging them to come around at all."
>
> "Oh, I didn't let him in the house. I remembered what you told me, and I went out, carefully shut the door, and looked at his things on the step. Besides, he wasn't an Italian—he was a German Jew. He had a big box full of very interesting things and he told me he was working hard to make enough money to bring his wife and children out from Germany. He spoke so feelingly about them that it touched my heart. I wanted to buy something from him to help him in such a worthy object."

In every village in every corner of the planet, we are likely to find a Marilla Cuthbert or a Mrs. Rachel Lynde—gatekeepers full of suspicion of and derision for the foreigner. But Anne's response humanizes the peddler and calls the reader to have compassion for his plight, giving us a good example of using differences between characters to counter xenophobia.

Sadly, though, the peddler cheats Anne in the end, and in other instances in Aunt Maud's writing, she uses the phrase "jewing down" to describe shrewd bargaining. The anti-Semitism of her culture crept into her work even though she may have tried to keep it out.

In *Looking for Anne of Green Gables: The Story of L. M. Montgomery and Her Literary Classic*, author Irene Gammel summarizes the cultural views of Aunt Maud's day as expressed in notes from the literary society to which she belonged. Members discussed "savage nations" and the "yellow peril" of Asians, for example. Gammel brings up another "bias in the bones of a book" issue: a deep-seated prejudice of English-speaking Canadians against the Acadian people on PEI who spoke French. "Even today North Rustico remains a vibrant Acadian settlement," writes Gammel. "Yet the Acadians are represented as being uneducated (the farmhand Jerry Buote), and stupid (the buxomy Mary Jo, an adult, appears to have less knowledge than Anne in treating little Minnie May Barry for croup). . . . The Acadians, the first settlers on Prince Edward Island, had suffered expulsion and expropriation, and were reclaiming their cultural rights during Maud's era. Buote was a respected Acadian name. . . . Maud's biases were those held by many English-speaking Canadians at the time."

When Marilla refers to "those stupid, half-grown little French boys," we can give Aunt Maud a pass thanks to the "bias in a character" card. But again, it's different when cultural stereotypes are expressed by an omniscient narrator or beloved protagonist like Anne.

If Aunt Maud and I were sitting together today, I would ask if she had considered how the book's portrayal of French-speaking Canadians might be received in Quebec or sound in translation into French. Given her sensitive spirit, the suffering she endured as a wife, and a dependence on prescription drugs that caused intense mental and physical anguish, I'm fairly sure she would be honest about her errors. Sadly, she grappled with those shortcomings at the end of her life. Her official cause of death was coronary thrombosis, but a questionable note was found by her bed that read, in part, "My position is too awful to endure and nobody realizes it. What an end to a life in which I tried always to do my best in spite of many mistakes."

I don't think Aunt Maud made this kind of "bias in the bones of a book" mistake in her portrayal of adoptees, another group of outsiders to PEI, but still, the negative view of them is jarring. When I read the book aloud to our nine-year-old twins, I wasn't seeing it through their eyes at first; I was simply sharing a book I had loved at their age. I froze, however, when I suddenly remembered what came next in the narrative.

Mrs. Lynde was about to declare that a "foreign orphan boy" would be of such an unknown quantity that he might suck eggs or poison the well with strychnine. Like the proverbial ton of bricks, it hit me. My own two beloved sons—"foreign orphan boys," in Mrs. Lynde's words—were going to take in a provincial, prejudiced woman's opinion about their adoption.

I stopped reading and looked at them. "What do you think of Mrs. Lynde?" I asked.

They thought about my question for a bit. Then "She's not a good guy," one of the boys answered.

"You're right," I said. "She's got some dumb ideas about other people. Let's keep reading and see if she changes by the end of the book."

As we read on past Mrs. Lynde's narrow-mindedness, we grasped the larger, more gracious message about adoption embedded deeply in the bones of the book. While Aunt Maud makes Anne's childhood suffering unstintingly clear, she portrays adoptees as much more than passive recipients of trauma who need rescue. Anne isn't "saved" by adoption in this book. Apart from growing older and talking a bit less, she doesn't actually transform much by the end of the story. Yes, Matthew and Marilla give her a home and family, but *they're* the ones who are changed by Anne more than the other way around. The adoptee as a powerful agent—now there's a message I was glad for my sons to hear.

Anne grows up through a series of books that feature her as the protagonist, in which Aunt Maud continued to honor the adoptee by including a thread of Anne's grief over losing her parents; her quest to return to her birthplace in Bolingbroke, Nova Scotia, in *Anne of the Island*; her joy in discovering letters written by her mother, Bertha Shirley; and a hint of the trauma of loss in *Anne of Windy Poplars*, where "in a few poignant sentences she sketch[es] her childhood before coming to Green Gables."

THE REAL HERO

Writing was a balm for Aunt Maud, who used her storytelling as a way to forgive her own elders in real life. Maybe that's why the *real* protagonist of this so-called children's book—a hero given an inciting incident and a journey of metanoia, or a transformative change of heart—is an adult: Marilla Cuthbert, the doyenne of Green Gables.

The first half of the book is fully told from Marilla's point of view. She and her brother, Matthew, lived for years without the presence of children before the arrival of Anne, an orphan from Nova Scotia. Apart from one passage describing internal despair, we are not privy to how Anne is processing the life-changing experience of being adopted at Green Gables. We see the events through Marilla's eyes alone as she begins to move from rigidity to love.

"Behind an attitude of rigidity, there is always something else in the life of a person," said Pope Francis. "Rigidity is not a gift of God. Meekness is, goodness is, benevolence is, forgiveness is. But rigidity isn't." In many cases, the pope continued, "rigidity conceals the leading of a double life, and there can also be something sick [behind it]." The human heart is prone to this sickness. One way to discern rigidity is to pay attention to internal reactions of contempt for other people. We ask ourselves this question: In what situations do I roll my eyes? This nonverbal thermometer reveals areas where I choose rigidity over love.

Saint Paul called love "the most excellent way" (1 Corinthians 12:31) and the greatest of all the spiritual gifts (1 Corinthians 13:13). In the year 388, Bishop Augustine of Hippo clarified the primacy of love in practicing the cardinal virtues: "Temperance is love giving itself entirely to that which is loved; fortitude is love readily bearing all things for the sake of the loved object; justice is love serving only the loved object, and therefore ruling rightly; prudence is love distinguishing with sagacity between what hinders it and what helps it." He makes love sound a lot like what we think of duty, doesn't he? In our culture, where the latter smacks of drudgery and rules, a closer look at love's destruction of Marilla's rigidity can reclaim the goodness of the word *duty*.

At the start of *Anne of Green Gables*, both Marilla the person and Green Gables the place are the perfect examples of rigidity. We meet them simultaneously in the first chapter through the eyes of a neighbor, Mrs. Rachel Lynde. Green Gables is isolated, set back from the road, built by a shy homesteader to be "as far away as he possibly could from his fellow men without actually retreating into the woods." The yard is "green and neat and precise," bordered by "patriarchal willows" and "prim Lombardies." It's so clean that Mrs. Lynde believes Marilla sweeps it as often as she sweeps the "painfully clean" house behind the yard.

Inside the kitchen, we meet Marilla, a tall, thin, angular woman who rarely sits and is "distrustful of sunshine." Her hair is "twisted up in a hard little knot behind with two wire hairpins stuck aggressively through it." She looks like a woman of "narrow experience and rigid conscience," but Aunt Maud offers the first indication of why we are supposed to root for this hero's journey: "There was a saving something about her mouth which, if it had been ever so slightly developed, might have been considered indicative of a sense of humor."

To Mrs. Lynde's amazement, Marilla informs her that they are adopting a boy. Marilla's reason for agreeing to her brother Matthew's desire to adopt is utilitarian: they want a boy "old enough to be of some use in doing chores right off and young enough to be trained up proper." They aren't going to exploit him—they "mean to give him a good home and schooling." Marilla sees it as her "duty to give in" because Matthew so rarely sets his mind on anything.

The house shows up again soon, but this time it's seen from a different perspective. Cue the dramatic encounter music, because this is big: Anne encounters Green Gables for the first time. She spots it with her home-hungry eyes even though it's "far back from the road, dimly white with blossoming trees in the twilight of the surrounding woods." Over the house, "a great crystal-white star was shining like a lamp of guidance and promise." She meets Marilla too. And then the older woman blurts out the terrible truth: they don't want Anne because she's a girl. Anne bursts into tears, and neither Marilla nor Matthew knows what to do until Marilla "step[s] lamely into the breach." Anne's arrival is an inciting incident, and the gesture of stepping forward is Marilla's first acceptance of the call to adventure—at least temporarily.

Now we see a hint of the change to come: a "reluctant smile, rather rusty from long disuse, mellowed Marilla's grim expression." But Green Gables, like Marilla, is not yet ready for transformation. The whitewashed walls and floor in the east gable room where Anne sleeps are "painfully bare and staring." "The whole apartment was of a rigidity not to be described in words," Aunt Maud writes. During her first night inside Green Gables, Anne cries herself to sleep.

Marilla also rejects a first invitation to metanoia, or profound transformation, which is typical in a hero's journey. She is wrathful at the turn of events and astonished that Matthew wants to keep Anne. "What good would she be to us?" Marilla asks. That's when Matthew issues the true call to love and sacrifice: "We might be some good to her." But "frowning most resolutely," Marilla refuses to acquiesce. What changes her mind?

MARILLA'S CALL TO ADVENTURE

Bit by bit, Marilla begins to recognize Anne's winsome personality. She mutters to herself, "She *is* kind of interesting, as Matthew says. I can feel already that I'm wondering what on earth she'll say next. She'll be casting a spell over me, too." But Anne's charm doesn't overcome Marilla's resistance; it's pity that does that. She (and we) hears Anne's backstory, which is a "life of drudgery and poverty and neglect." For the first time in the narrative, Marilla considers keeping Anne.

The etymology of *pity* reveals the word's proximity to duty and piety, both of which relate to the idea of vocation. *Pity* comes from the Old French word *pite*, which referred to "mercy, compassion, care, tenderness [for another's] pitiful state or wretched condition." It also has roots in the Latin *pietatem*, which refers to "piety, loyalty, duty."

Pity is beginning to motivate Marilla to accept a new vocation: motherhood. But there isn't enough yet in her heart to move her to adopt Anne. The appearance of Mrs. Peter Blewett, a notoriously cruel Avonlea resident who is seeking a girl to look after her many children, seals the deal. When Mrs. Spencer, who had accidentally brought a girl instead of a boy from the orphanage as the Cuthberts requested, sees Mrs. Blewett as the perfect remedy for the dilemma, she calls it "positively providential." Marilla, however, "did not look as if she thought Providence had much to do with the matter." The word *Providence* isn't dropped into the narrative lightly. When capitalized, it means "God conceived as the power sustaining and guiding human destiny." Is this destiny? God's plan for Anne? For Marilla? The reader is nudged to ask those questions because providentially, at that opportune moment, Mrs. Blewett enters the story.

Now we come to the point of no return that is typical in a hero's journey. Thanks to pity and to Providence, Marilla decides to do something irrevocable: "Marilla looked at Anne and softened at the sight of the child's pale face with its look of mute misery. . . . [She] felt an uncomfortable conviction that if she denied the appeal of that look, it would haunt her to her dying day. . . . No, she could not take the responsibility of doing that!" Later, in the yard behind the barn at Green Gables, she announces to Matthew her decision to keep Anne: "I've been thinking over the idea until I've got kind of used to it. It seems a sort of duty. I've never brought up a child, especially a girl, and I dare say I'll make a terrible mess of it. But I'll do my best."

Let the adventure begin! Our hero has accepted the invitation to begin her journey of duty and love.

LOVE MAKES MARILLA A MOTHER

Soon we find Marilla feeling a "most reprehensible desire to laugh" when she's with Anne. Her sense of humor is developing, but she is still in strict control of her emotions until Anne slips her hand into Marilla's to declare her allegiance to Green Gables: "I never loved any place before. No place ever seemed like home." Marilla's move toward motherly love begins here: "Something warm and pleasant welled up in Marilla's heart at the touch of that thin little hand in her own—a throb of the maternity she had missed, perhaps. Its very unaccustomedness and sweetness disturbed her." This bubbling-up of emotion is disconcerting for our hero, and outwardly, she remains crisp and rigid. But then Marilla has a moment of deep self-reflection and awareness, wondering if her own secret critical (but truthful) thoughts about church were taking form "in the person of this outspoken morsel of neglected humanity."

Even after Marilla tells Anne of their decision to keep her, Anne is afraid that she might be returned to the orphanage. After an outburst of anger over a perceived insult to her looks and subsequent apology to Mrs. Lynde, Anne probes Marilla outright to see if this newfound love is conditional. "Maybe you'd better send me back to the asylum," she suggests with tears after Marilla's irritation over Anne's adorning of her churchgoing hat with flowers. "Nonsense," Marilla responds crisply. "I don't want to send you back to the asylum, I'm sure." This is the bright side of a rigid, unimaginative, unemotional personality—Anne has learned already that Marilla always means what she says. She honestly *wants* to keep Anne; she wouldn't just say this to please the hearer. Now Anne can endure what comes next—Marilla's suspicion of her new ward's dishonesty in the matter of a lost amethyst brooch. But when Anne is vindicated, Marilla commends her generosity to Matthew. She even confesses that she's "glad she consented to keep the child" and is "getting fond of her."

Then comes a big moment: Anne voluntarily kisses Marilla for the first time. "There, there," Marilla says curtly in response. But we are privy to her innermost feelings: "Again that sudden sensation of startling sweetness thrilled her. She was secretly vastly pleased at Anne's impulsive caress." Soon, this growing inward affection is seen by others. Marilla admits to Matthew that she has made a mistake and affirms that Anne is going to turn out "all right." Although we've previously seen hints of Marilla's humor in a twitching mouth or another subtle, self-controlled nonverbal cue, we see her bursting into "such a hearty and unusual peal of laughter" that Matthew overhears. Stunned, he wonders when he'd ever heard his sister laugh like that before.

Deep change is taking place. Marilla lifts a loose curl of hair from Anne's sleeping face and kisses "the flushed cheek on the pillow." From that point on, the chapters move to Anne's point of view, and Marilla shifts more into the backdrop as a maternal confidante and teacher. There's one exception of a shift back into Marilla's perspective, when

Anne is injured falling off the Barrys' fence. If you have the book nearby, hold the novel open to this pivotal moment—it arrives in what is almost the center of the story. Marilla sees Mr. Barry coming up the slope carrying Anne, "whose head lay limply against his shoulder." Instantly, the writer takes us deep into Marilla's internal emotional condition. It's not pity—it's fear: "In the sudden stab of fear that pierced to her very heart she realized what Anne had come to mean to her. She would have admitted that she liked Anne—nay, that she was very fond of Anne. But now she knew as she hurried wildly down the slope that Anne was dearer to her than anything on earth."

Author Brené Brown points out fear's connection to *vulnerability*, a word that originates in the Latin *vulnerare* and can be defined as "capable of being wounded." Marilla is now capable of being wounded; she has become fully vulnerable thanks to her love of Anne. From that point on, the older woman's emotions range from anxiety to pride to tenderness to a vested, intense caring—all the normal feelings of a loving mother. And tears, too, which assuredly come with the role. "Whenever you find tears in your eyes, especially unexpected tears, it is well to pay the closest attention," writes Frederick Buechner. At the start of the book, it is forlorn Anne who sobs passionately and unreservedly. At the end, it is Marilla who breaks down and weeps bitterly. Rigidity has become love.

When Matthew dies (sorry—huge spoiler), Marilla loses the last of her close genetic relatives. She is an orphan without siblings, just like Anne, whose longing for filial relationships is expressed early in the story. "I've never had an aunt or any relation at all—not even a grandmother," she tells Marilla, asking how her new guardian wants to be addressed. "It would make me feel as if I really belonged to you." Marilla tells her brusquely to call her by her first name, which Anne does. But who cares about a title? By the end of the novel, the two are bonded into family. Marilla gathers a grieving Anne in her arms, confessing how much she loves "her girl, her joy and comfort," as much as if Anne "were her own flesh and blood." Anne has become the beloved daughter of a mother.

Green Gables the house has also changed, mirroring Marilla's transformation: "The east gable room was a very different place from what it had been on that night four years before, when Anne had felt its bareness penetrate to the marrow of her spirit with its inhospitable chill. Changes had crept in, Marilla conniving at them resignedly, until it was as sweet and dainty a nest as a young girl could desire." The mother has provided a nest, and a shared love of Green Gables motivates Anne to save it for both of them.

THE INTERTWINING OF LOVE AND DUTY

Just as Marilla began her relationship with Anne out of duty, Anne in turn seals their familial bond with a dutiful act. Anne retreats to (where else?) that transformed east gable room to make her difficult choice: "Before she went to bed there was a smile on her lips and peace in her heart. She had looked her duty courageously in the face and found it a friend—as duty ever is when we meet it frankly."

She relinquishes her dream of going away for higher education to prevent Green Gables from being sold. While Marilla's decision to keep Anne was motivated by pity for a stranger, Anne's dutiful act to remain with Marilla is driven by love. In both cases, duty is linked to love—Marilla's dutiful choice leads to love, while Anne's stems from it. It takes time for Marilla to reap the rewards of her choice because her love for Anne has to grow; Anne immediately begins to enjoy the satisfaction of laying down her life for someone she already deeply loves.

One of my favorite themes in *Anne of Green Gables* is the illumination of how love between a powerful person and a powerless person can change the former for the better. "What good would she be to us?" Marilla asks Mathew at the start of her hero's journey. A lot of good, it turns out. As a love of Anne transforms rigid, unemotional Marilla, so we as readers are invited to be changed by our love for this sweet, passionate girl. Thanks to the bond forged between two of Aunt Maud's most endearing characters, Green Gables remains a fictional home for generations of readers around the world. Steep your soul in it over several rereads, and the love in this novel is bound to shape your spiritual journey.

REFLECT AND DISCUSS

1. How do you connect with Anne's character? Is there anything you especially admire about her?

2. Name a place on the planet that feels like home to you. Describe it with all five senses.

3. When is the last time you've rolled your eyes at someone, internally or externally? Does this reveal an area of rigidity in your heart to be confessed? How might you seek to love that person in your next interaction?

4. Which dutiful decision to sacrifice—Marilla's (prompted by pity for a stranger) or Anne's (motivated by love)—seems more difficult?

5. Like Marilla, we discover the depth of our loves by the extent of fear over their possible loss. What or whom do you most fear losing?

6. Do you have a deep relationship in your life with someone less powerful in society? If so, with whom? How did it form? If not, is there some way to cross a border of power to increase the chances of developing such a transformational relationship?

4
ᴀLIENATION
AND FᴀITH

HEIDI BY JOHANNA SPYRI

I am more happy than I deserve; to be at peace with God
and men makes one's heart feel light.

—the Alm-Uncle

Heidi is one of the best-selling books ever written. It was
originally published in 1881 in two parts—as *Heidi:
Her Years of Wandering and Learning* and *Heidi: How She Used
What She Learned*. This novel, about a winsome orphan raised
by her paternal grandfather in the Swiss Alps, is "for children
and those who love children," as the author, Johanna Spyri

(Tante Johanna), made clear in the book's original subtitle. Sadly, when I mention the novel these days, most children have never read it. If grown-ups have heard of it, they think of a blonde Shirley Temple or a young mountain miss on a hot chocolate logo.

Heidi may have fallen out of circulation in the West, but the novel is still read widely in Asia by adults and children alike. Heidiland in Switzerland, an amusement park based on the novel, caters mostly to Japanese and Korean tourists, and a Japanese animated series based on the book became wildly popular in several Asian countries. The novel is beloved in India as well. Novelist and poet Deepa Agarwal wrote about her adoration of the book in the *Indian Express*: "When Heidi came into my hands as a nine-year-old, I was enthralled by this little girl's ability to transform so many people, bring sunshine into so many lives . . . when we visited the charming museum that has been set up in Spyri's old schoolhouse in the picturesque village of Hirzel, the sight of her family home, her grandfather's house and the church she must have attended, literally gave me goosebumps!"

I understand her rapture. This story about a girl in the Swiss Alps was immensely appealing to a young Bengali immigrant on a fire escape in Flushing. Did it resonate with my longing for the rural quiet of my father's ancestral village, which he always described with fond nostalgia, as I looked out at a city of noise, concrete, and crowds? As with *Anne of*

Green Gables, was it the honor given to the elderly, a value my parents instilled in us from birth? My grandparents lived on the other side of the world, and I grew up without their presence in my life. Was I drawn to Tante Johanna's portrayal of the filial love of a child who chooses a rustic life with a grandparent over luxuries in a stranger's home?

I imagine it was all of these. Today, when I reread the story, what I find most intriguing is the depiction of a transformation from the alienation of broken relationships to the homecoming of faith.

OUR NEED TO BELONG

Belonging is a powerful, fundamental, and extremely pervasive motivation. Psychologists Roy Baumeister and Mark Leary found in a 1995 study that satisfying this need requires (a) frequent, positive interactions with the same individuals and (b) engaging in these interactions within a framework of long-term, stable care and concern. A sense of belongingness is crucial to well-being, Baumeister and Leary argued. People who lack it suffer higher levels of mental and physical illness and are more prone to a broad range of behavioral problems, ranging from traffic accidents to criminality to suicide.

Loneliness has grown exponentially since that study, especially in more prosperous cities and countries. Researchers now identify the three most lonely stages of our lives: in the late twenties, a time of high stress and difficult decisions; in the midfifties, when we face declining vigor and midlife crises; and in the late eighties, when we endure the deaths of spouses, siblings, and friends.

Bad news, I thought when I discovered this. Our sons are in the first stage, my husband and I are smack-dab in the second, and our elderly mothers are moving into the third. To counter some of this loneliness, we recently made changes in jobs and housing to be within walking distance of both Ma and our boys. When I borrow an egg from the boys' cottage and deliver it to my mother for a recipe, it feels eerily like a return to the multigenerational jute farm of my ancestors.

Not everyone is as fortunate. In the United Kingdom, after defining loneliness as a public health crisis, former Prime Minister Theresa May appointed the country's first "minister for loneliness." Here in the United States, a study found that social isolation is "associated with a reduction in lifespan similar to that caused by smoking 15 cigarettes a day." We middle-aged people are so lonely that our suicide rates are rising dangerously. The elderly are also experiencing deep isolation and alienation. In Japan, some older people are so desperate to combat loneliness that they commit petty crimes in order to find company in jail. They fear *kodokushi*, a new Japanese term that means a lonely death detected only when neighbors begin to smell decomposition.

Perhaps the oddest turn of events in our era is the deepening of loneliness among young adults, a time in life that used to be the most socially engaged. A study by the health company Cigna found that more than half of young adults in the United States feel left out or isolated. Those who use social media more than two hours a day have twice the chance of experiencing social anxiety, and those who access it fifty or more times a week have three times the odds of perceived social isolation as those who use social media fewer than nine times a week. The study also found that 69 percent of people in this age group felt that the people around them were "not really with them," and 68 percent felt as if no one knew them well.

This epidemic of loneliness is spreading in other continents. Throughout cities in Asia, for example, where more and more people in their twenties and thirties are living and working alone, demand is growing for solo karaoke booths and restaurant seating for one. Thinking of these young people eating and singing alone grieves my heart.

WHY SO LONELY?

Even as sociologists and psychologists try to shed light on this growing sense of alienation, you may have your own theories about what is causing it. Here are mine. First, many of us have left behind villages of origin and extended families.

Were you born in the same town as your great-grandparents? Probably not. Do you live close to extended family? Again, it's likely that you don't. The fact that we don't live near kin makes us lonelier than people in other times and places.

As I said earlier, my parents both grew up in multigenerational homes, as is common in the villages of Bengal. A child in that context quickly learns specific familial terms in Bangla used to reveal relational connection. Instead of the more generic word *uncle*, for example, I called my mother's youngest brother Chotomama, while my father's older brother was my Jehtu, and so on. If I introduced you to a woman named Mejomaima, you would know just by the moniker that she was married to the second of my mother's three brothers. The Bengali language makes room for the specifics of a kin network much more than English does, which only offers generic terms like *uncle* and *aunt*. As an immigrant, though, I didn't reap the benefits of having these beloved elders as a part of daily life. I missed them; I still do. If we'd all stayed in the village, it's likely we'd be deeply interconnected.

During the twentieth century, as people like us immigrated and others moved from rural areas of the United States into suburbs and cities, one of the replacements for kin networks were faith communities. Places of worship linked strangers into family who supported each other, and weekly gatherings over years cemented close friendships. With religious affiliation plummeting in the twenty-first century, many of us no longer have such covenantal connections.

A separation from family and faith communities becomes even more drastic when one or both were not safe havens. We may be battling bitterness toward those who have disagreed with us, done harm, or sat in judgment over us. Amy Banks, a psychiatrist and author of *Wired to Connect*, describes this state: "When people are chronically disconnected, or in a relationship that has a chronic disconnection . . . [they] have no energy; there's almost a paralysis. They start getting confused about whose issue is this—is it mine, is it yours? So clarity is gone, and you feel bad about yourself. You feel like, I have to protect myself, I feel like I have to be even more isolated. All of the things that go up in a good relationship completely tank in a bad one."

Around us and inside our own hearts, we sense a desperate, unnamed desire for belonging and reconciliation, both to God and to other human beings. Writer Frederick Buechner wrote about this in *The Longing for Home*: "The word longing comes from the same root as the word long in the sense of length in either time or space and also the word belong, so that in its full richness to long suggests to yearn for a long time for something that is a long way off and something that we feel we belong to and that belongs to us. The longing for home is so universal a form of longing that there is even a special word for it, which is, of course homesickness."

It is the virtue of faith that allows us to move from the alienation of homesickness to the belonging of home. And that's exactly what we see in Tante Johanna's novel.

THE ALM-UNCLE'S ALIENATION

Peter; the goatherd's grandmother, Heidi's closest neighbor on the mountain; Clara, a wealthy but sick girl living in Frankfurt; and Clara's doctor, who also lives in the city: all are lonely before Heidi enters their lives. The grandmother is lonely because of poverty and neglect, Clara's loneliness stems from her illness, and the doctor is grieving the loss of his daughter. While these experiences are deeply painful, loneliness resulting from broken relationships is the most heartbreaking loneliness of all, as Dr. Banks discovered in her research on chronic disconnection. Damaged relationships are why Tante Johanna's most desolate character—the one who dominates the narrative arc of the novel—is Heidi's paternal grandfather, the Alm-Uncle.

Like the wild and raucous bird that dwells alone on the mountain, the Alm-Uncle has shunned human connection for five years. Bitter and brokenhearted, he is alienated from family, neighbors, and God. Heidi's maternal aunt Deta shares his history at the start of the novel, describing how he returned to his hometown after squandering his inheritance. With a history of selfishness and rumors of a criminal history dogging him, he received no welcome in the place of his roots. "Embittered by this treatment, he vowed never to set foot in Domleschg again," Deta informs a curious acquaintance. But even in Dörfli, where he settled next, the townspeople looked on him with suspicion.

Tragedy struck again when a falling beam killed the Alm-Uncle's son Tobias, and his daughter-in-law Adelaide died shortly afterward. According to Deta, the people saw it as "a punishment that Uncle had deserved for the godless life he had led," and "some went so far even to tell him so to his face." (A judgmental faith community full of people who let loose with their tongues? Some things never change.) "One minister endeavored to awaken his conscience and exhorted him to repentance, but the old man grew only more wrathful and obdurate and would not speak to a soul," Deta says as she climbs the mountain toward where the old man has been living in solitude for five years. She is determined to leave her sister's orphaned child, Heidi, with the girl's paternal grandfather; there's no other way to accept a dream job offer.

Imagine the Alm-Uncle's state of mind when a bustling young woman, with Heidi in tow, invades his desolation. Heidi reaches him first and goes "straight up to the old man, put[s] out her hand, and [says], 'Good-evening, Grandfather.'" By calling him grandfather, she establishes their connection and kinship. Now he knows her identity.

He gives her hand an abrupt shake, and the two take stock of each other, Heidi's gaze unflinching and steady.

How would you feel if after five years of solitude, nursing deep hurt and bitterness, a small child shows up to claim you as her relative, and you are required to care for her indefinitely? When the Alm-Uncle hears of Deta's plan to leave Heidi with him, he is furious. He predicts that Heidi will "fret and whine" and describes her (and other children) as one of "these unreasonable human beings."

Once Deta leaves, Tante Johanna tells us that the old man "went back to his bench, and there he remained seated," no longer gazing at the view but "staring on the ground without uttering a sound." He is disturbed; his life is upended. As was the case with Marilla in *Anne of Green Gables*, the advent of an unwanted child is a call to adventure.

FAMILY TIES

It doesn't take Heidi long to win the Alm-Uncle over—only one day and night. In their first encounter alone, she tells her grandfather that she doesn't want the city clothes Deta sent with her. The Alm-Uncle turns and looks "searchingly at the child, whose dark eyes were sparkling," and notes her intelligence. Working together, they shape her a bed out of hay and coarse sackcloth. When Heidi asks for a coverlid, her grandfather suspects that the "whining and fretting" will begin, but Heidi's easygoing response puts that fear to rest. "Well, never mind, grandfather," she says in a consoling tone of voice. "I can take some more hay to put over me."

Her grandfather provides instead a thick sack, and once he is finished helping her shape the bed, Heidi is delighted with her new nest. Next, she relishes the meal he provides, drinking the bowl of goat's milk in one gulp. "Was the milk nice?" he asks. "I never drank any so good before," answers Heidi, looking the "picture of content." This child is not a complainer, the Alm-Uncle is beginning to see.

When he makes her a stool of her own, she responds with astonishment and admiration. How must that feel to an old man who has had nobody to appreciate his skills in cooking and carpentry? How must it be to have her shadowing him "step by step, her eyes attentively taking in all that he did, and everything that she saw was a fresh source of pleasure to her?"

And then come the goats. "Are they ours, Grandfather?" Heidi asks in glee. *Ours*—a beautiful word of appropriation for property shared by family. Here is his chance to disenfranchise this child from shared ownership of his property with a curt, "They are mine." But "Yes, yes," the old man says, affirming her filial invitation.

At the close of that first day of upheaval and change, a tempestuous wind comes howling, breaking branches and storming with fury—the perfect metaphor for what has happened in Alm-Uncle's soul. He decides to check on the child, assuming she will be frightened. Instead, he finds her "with a happy expression on her baby face as if dreaming of something pleasant." Tante Johanna tells us that the "old man stood looking down on the sleeping child until the moon again disappeared behind the cloud and he could see no more."

Now the two are inseparable.

HEIDI'S DEPARTURE

The Alm-Uncle, however, is still intent on staying apart from others and from God, keeping Heidi for three years on the mountain away from school and church. When a pastor visits and asks him to consider bringing Heidi down to the village to live during the winters, the Alm-Uncle makes it clear he has no intention to be reconciled with God or neighbor:

> "I couldn't live in the village, for the people there and I despise each other; we had better keep apart."
>
> "You are mistaken, I assure you! Make your peace with God, and then you'll see how happy you will be."
>
> The clergyman had risen, and holding out his hand, he said cordially: "I shall count on you next winter, neighbor. We shall receive you gladly, reconciled with God and man."

But the uncle replied firmly, while he shook his visitor by the hand: "Thank you for your kindness, but you will have to wait in vain."

"God be with you," said the parson, and left him sadly.

The Alm-Uncle's relationship with Heidi is enough for him; he adores her by now. Picture, then, how he feels when Deta returns again, this time to take away the granddaughter he has come to cherish. The two grown-ups have a fierce argument in a scene that is the narrative's darkest moment:

Deta, flaming up, replied: "Do you want to hear what I think? Don't I know how old she is; eight years old and ignorant of everything. They have told me that you refuse to send her to church and to school. She is my only sister's child, and I shall not bear it, for I am responsible. You do not care for her, how else could you be indifferent to such luck. You had better give way or I shall get the people to back me. If I were you, I would not have it brought to court; some things might be warmed up that you would not care to hear about."

"Be quiet!" the uncle thundered with flaming eyes. "Take her and ruin her, but do not bring her before my sight again. I do not want to see her with feathers in her hat and wicked words like yours."

Heidi is tricked into accompanying her aunt, leaving the Alm-Uncle more bitter and lonely than before her arrival: "From that day forward Alm-Uncle looked fiercer and more forbidding than ever . . . he spoke to no one, and looked such an ogre as he came along with his pack of cheese on his back, his immense stick in his hand, and his thick, frowning eyebrows, that the women would call to their little ones, 'Take care! Get out of Alm-Uncle's way or he may hurt you!'"

HEIDI FINDS FAITH

One of the strangest phenomena of belief is that difficulties can deepen instead of diminish it. Exiled, alienated, and virtually imprisoned in Frankfurt, far from home and family, Heidi endures loneliness and separation. During this time of trial, however, she learns to read, hears the parable of the prodigal son, and is given the gift of faith. She leaves Frankfurt with a devout belief that despite sorrow and hardship, divine love never fails. In a paradox that holds true in every age and culture, suffering enables her to become an agent of reconciliation for her beloved grandfather.

Heidi's conviction that there is a good, loving God deepens once she returns to the mountain. She learns more about spiritual life from the hymns she reads aloud to Peter's grandmother, who is herself a model of faith despite her suffering. In this novel about belief, Tante Johanna even tackles the hard question of theodicy, creating a scene for Heidi to use a hymn in answering the question of why a good God permits the manifestation of evil. "But if it is God Himself who has sent the trouble, what can we say to Him then?" asks the doctor, crushed by the death of his daughter. Heidi doesn't give a quick response to his question; instead, she sits in silence, thinking deeply. The answer that eventually comes is devout and trusting, but when her theology doesn't convince the doctor of God's love, she asks if she may recite one of Peter's grandmother's hymns. The doctor assents, and the words remind him of his childhood and of his mother, bringing a measure of comfort to his troubled heart.

Heidi's return to the mountain—a second coming of sorts—catalyzes the Alm-Uncle's complete transformation. Writing about their reunion, Tante Johanna places him once again on that lonely bench. He knows Heidi has overheard Deta's words about his past and that his granddaughter now realizes what kind of a man he is. He understands how three years of living as a stranger in a sophisticated city can harden a person's heart. And yet here comes Heidi, racing up the mountain to him, making it clear she's been longing for him every moment she's been away: "Now she could see her grandfather sitting on his bench, smoking a pipe. Above the cottage the fir-trees gently swayed and rustled in the evening breeze. At last she had reached the hut, and throwing herself in her grandfather's arms, she hugged him and held him tight. She could say nothing but 'Grandfather! grandfather! grandfather!' in her agitation. The old man said nothing either, but his eyes were moist, and loosening Heidi's arms at last, he sat her on his knee."

After they reestablish their life together, Heidi shares with him Jesus's story of forgiveness. She describes God as a parent who waits patiently, yearning after a wayward child. No matter how much theology she shares with her grandfather, however, I doubt he could have imagined a God of love racing to embrace him if his granddaughter hadn't done so first. Because of Heidi's love, the story of the merciful father can penetrate the Alm-Uncle's heart. Later, when he is alone, he responds to the prodigal son's homecoming with tears of repentance and a prayer of confession: "A few hours later, when Heidi was sleeping soundly, the old man climbed up the ladder. Placing a little lamp beside the sleeping child, he watched her a long, long time. Her little hands were folded and her rosy face looked confident and peaceful. The old man now folded his hands and said in a low voice, while big tears rolled down his cheeks: 'Father, I have sinned against Heaven and Thee, and am no more worthy to be Thy son!'"

THE ALM-UNCLE IS RESTORED TO SERVE

But a private confession to God isn't enough. A person must return to the community of faith as part of confession, as

Dietrich Bonhoeffer made clear in *Life Together*: "In confession the breakthrough to community takes place. Sin demands to have a man by himself. It withdraws him from the community. The more isolated a person is, the more destructive will be the power of sin over him, and the more deeply he becomes involved in it, the more disastrous is his isolation."

The story Jesus told of a father with two sons doesn't end with paternal delight over the younger son's return. It continues with an invitation to a restored relationship between the brothers. The Alm-Uncle must make amends with others in his faith community, even though they have acted like the judgmental older brother to his prodigal son.

And so the old man heads down the mountain with Heidi on Sunday morning. They join the congregation to worship, and afterward, the Alm-Uncle confesses to the pastor he had rejected earlier in the story: "I have come to ask your forgiveness for my harsh words." The other man generously gives it. Church members, stirred by Heidi's obvious and deep love for her grandfather, follow their pastor's lead with grace:

> The pastor's friendly eyes sparkled, and with many a kind word he commended the uncle for this change, and putting his hand on Heidi's curly hair, ushered them out. Thus the people, who had been all talking together about this great event, could see that their clergyman shook hands with the old man. The door of the parsonage was hardly shut, when the whole

assembly came forward with outstretched hands and friendly greetings. Great seemed to be their joy at the old man's resolution; some of the people even accompanied him on his homeward way. When they had parted at last, the uncle looked after them with his face shining as with an inward light.

Reconciled with God and neighbor, the Alm-Uncle may now serve as a partner to Heidi in the healing of Clara and the doctor. An ability to care for the sick, learned during suffering in his past, and a deep knowledge of the ecology of the mountain, acquired during years of isolation, are redeemed and put to use in a new life of faith. By the end of the story, the Alm-Uncle spends half the year in town to enable Heidi to attend school and is firmly entrenched as a valued member of the community.

HEIDI SHARES HER FAITH

What does Heidi do to help reconnect her alienated grandfather to faith, community, and service? Her fourfold strategy is a beautiful one to emulate, especially in our culture of alienation.

First, Heidi is attentive to whatever is noble, excellent, and praiseworthy in her grandfather's life. May we, too, seek to affirm goodness and offer a loving, admiring gaze in our encounters with lonely people.

Second, Heidi makes it clear that she enjoys and even delights in his company. From the smallest child to an elder afflicted with dementia, human beings discern when a person truly wants to be with them: "I've learned that people will forget what you said, people will forget what you did, but people will never forget how you made them feel." This anonymous quote, often misattributed to the poet Maya Angelou, sums up Heidi's gift.

Third, Heidi believes in God's expansive capacity to forgive. While Tante Johanna makes it clear in her writing that Heidi overhears her aunt's insinuations about her grandfather's past, Heidi never asks for details. She knows him. She knows, as Bryan Stevenson puts it in *Just Mercy*, his book about people on death row, that "each of us is more than the worst thing we've ever done." Heidi, too, believes in a God of grace who welcomes anyone who confesses. Like a better version of an elder brother, who was culturally responsible in Jesus's day for the well-being of younger siblings, she goes out to find the younger brother and bring him home.

Last but not least, there's the mystery of how suffering makes us useful in the spiritual journey of another. It is Heidi's season of loneliness that enables her to bring reconciliation into her grandfather's life. So, too, may our deepest sorrows serve others one day. As the Alm-Uncle affirms the deeper purpose of Heidi's time of exile, we yearn for the redemption of our seasons of loneliness: "It is always Sunday with us now; Heidi has not been away in vain."

REFLECT AND DISCUSS

1. Do you live close to kin? What is your relationship like with extended family?

2. Did you grow up as part of a faith community? What was that experience like?

3. Where and to whom do you belong deeply now? List people, groups, and communities.

4. Have you been alienated from or bitter toward a group to which you used to belong or a person you once loved? What was the cause? Is there any hope of reconciliation?

5. Which one of the four "Heidi faith-building strategies" are you pursuing at this point in your spiritual life: being present, seeking virtue in encounters, believing in grace for all those who want to change, or enduring alienation yourself?

6. Think of a person in your life who seems lonely. What is a change you might make in your interactions with that person?

5

ᴅᴇSPAIR AND ᴴOPE

EMILY OF DEEP VALLEY BY MAUD HART LOVELACE

Muster your wits; stand in your own defense.

—Emily Webster

It didn't take long for that immigrant reader on the fire escape (me) to discover another author named Maud in the public library: Maud Hart Lovelace. For clarity's sake, let's call Lucy Maud Montgomery, the author of *Anne of Green Gables*, Aunt Maud and this writer Auntie Maud. Auntie Maud's classic Betsy-Tacy series served as a superb orientation for a newcomer eager to understand the history and heritage of the United States. Those books took me back to the early 1900s, when many of the values that resonated in my old-world home—thrift, duty, community, respect for elders—still animated American life, but they also sparkled with timeless humor that made me laugh out loud. I was starting to see that the best stories blended three main ingredients: people, place, and plot. Auntie Maud's books had all three, and her characters easily danced off the pages into my friend-hungry heart.

I finished the "high school" Betsy-Tacy books first, when the characters who start as small girls in the series become teenagers, and immediately added Betsy to my growing list of fictional best buddies. Then in *Emily of Deep Valley*, Auntie Maud introduced me to Emily Webster, a girl who attended the same high school as Betsy. This novel is full of familiar characters—robust Bobby Cobb, stately Miss Bangeter, fun-loving Cab Edwards, and petite, dark-eyed Miss Fowler, Deep Valley's treasure of an English teacher. Alice, Dennie, Winona, Tacy, Tib, and even Betsy herself make an appearance in the book, but all of them play supporting minor roles in what is indisputably Emily's story.

With each subsequent read, I root for Emily from the first pages of this novel. She is treasurer of her class and a master debater—the only girl on an all-guy team who helps her school win the Southern Minnesota Championship two years in a row. Even though she's an orphan—yes, this is the third orphan in a row we're meeting, and all three live with elderly people—Emily isn't jealous of her popular, pretty second cousin's doting parents. She sticks to her own classic, simple style when it comes to clothes and doesn't try to imitate Annette's frills and lace. And while some of her peers scoff at tradition, Emily rises early to decorate the graves of her ancestors, dutifully pressing her grandfather's uniform and esteeming the old Gettysburg soldiers marching on Decoration Day. When Miss Fowler suggests a housekeeper to take care of her grandfather so that Emily can go to college, Emily's loyal, self-sacrificial answer comes quickly: "No. He's eighty-one. I've lived with him all my life."

DESPAIR ABOUNDING

Despite these strengths, Emily has relatable flaws. She's shy and socially awkward, has low self-esteem, and battles despondency as she faces a future without college or family. Her all-too-human struggle with sadness resonates deeply in a time when so many of us feel our own future is bleak. According to a recent Pew Research Center survey, 60 percent of American adults think that the United States will be less powerful in three decades. Almost two-thirds say the country will be even more divided politically. Fifty-nine percent think the environment will deteriorate. Nearly three-quarters say that the gap between people with more wealth and people with less wealth will widen. Most of us expect the average family's standard of living to decline.

"Hope deferred makes the heart sick," said the writer of Proverbs (13:12). We see this all around us, with people experiencing historical highs in heartsickness, manifesting as depression, anxiety, addiction, and suicide. Rates of depression among kids ages fourteen to seventeen have all increased substantially in recent times, along with suicidal thoughts, plans, and attempts, which in some cases more than doubled, one study found.

Psychiatrist Jean Twenge posits that this mental health crisis is due to the ubiquitous presence of smartphones, a technology that magnifies bullying, sleep deprivation, and the fear of missing out. "For all their power to link kids day and night, social media also exacerbate the age-old teen concern about being left out," she writes. "Today's teens may go to fewer parties and spend less time together in person, but when they do congregate, they document their hangouts relentlessly. . . . Those not invited to come along are keenly aware of it. Accordingly, the number of teens who feel left out has reached all-time highs across age groups. Like the increase in loneliness, the upswing in feeling left out has been swift and significant."

The internet isn't content with making despair worse for teens; it is demoralizing most of us no matter our age. A constant barrage on our attention, 24-7 access to terrifying news, divisions magnified by social media—all of it deepens our despondency.

The power of reading a story from the past, though, is that it reminds us of a truth: we human beings don't change much at the core, despite our trappings. Take Emily, for example. In the days before smartphones, she experienced all three things linked to them: a fear of missing out, bullying, and sleep issues. As the senior girls in her crowd head off to college, we feel her desolation on the train platform. When they return, full of news about sororities, fraternities, and other kinds of college fun and learning, she feels more left out than ever. Bullying existed back then too. Isn't Don—the classmate and fellow debate team member who is Emily's secret crush—basically a narcissist who takes pleasure in Emily's feelings of inferiority? And there's nothing new about sleep deprivation's connection to mental health. Emily cries in her room alone at night, and after enduring rejection and despair at a Christmas gathering, she wakes before the light feeling like something terrible had happened. She tries to press "her arm across her eyes to hold it back, but it came—the detestable memory . . . !"

Depression is next—a state of mind that Auntie Maud understood and perhaps even experienced herself in the years before doctors began diagnosing it as a treatable condition: "'A mood like this has to be fought. It's like an enemy with a gun,' [Emily] told herself. But she couldn't seem to find a gun with which to fight." The book's descriptions of the malady ring true, as when Emily is feeling empty and lifeless, her mind reaching out for anything to fill the day, or when she bends her head in her arms and believes the future holds nothing but sorrow. Her grandfather watches anxiously, walking on eggshells because of her condition. And the metaphorical use of Emily's "slough of Despond" is apt: "The sky was covered with low-hanging clouds but she could see the slough, frozen into a sea of hard brown billows. Except for a line of untidy muskrat houses, there wasn't a sign of life in that desolate place."

DASHED DREAMS

This fictional depiction of despondency that took place a century ago is oddly comforting today. If you've ever longed for something and not received it, or loved someone who doesn't return that love, *Emily of Deep Valley* is the story for you.

One of Emily's dreams is to study sociology. She admires Jane Addams and longs to help the poor, but she can't see a way to accomplish her dream without higher education. She also desires Don, her second cousin Annette's significant other, but he doesn't return her affection. Her dashed dreams lead to despondency.

Ours do too. Think about a desire you've had to let go of—a door that stayed closed no matter how much you wanted to walk through it. A friend of mine who escaped persecution in her home country, for example, is waiting for her children and husband to join her in the United States. Their request for asylum has been denied repeatedly, no matter how much we beseech God or ask politicians to intervene. Other friends are seeking healing from disease—healing that doesn't come in spite of excellent medical care and a massive, concerted rallying of prayer.

Some of our unfulfilled desires seem "smaller" by comparison, but measuring them against other people's losses doesn't seem to minimize their hard slam in the soul. Maybe there was a job you wanted, admission to a school, a baby, another baby, a person you longed to marry, a job or a spouse for someone you love . . . the list of dreams that never come true grows longer as decades go by.

The poet Langston Hughes poignantly described a life of dead dreams as "a broken-winged bird." We try to numb the pain with substances, entertainment, and other distractions, but that doesn't seem to work. We strive to empty ourselves of desire but soon realize that we're designed for deep attachment no matter how much we meditate or breathe. Soon despondency takes the wheel and we *do* get numb, we *do* stop desiring anything, and discover that we're stuck in a life devoid of hope. "Living without hope is like no longer living," wrote the German theologian Jürgen Moltmann. Sadly, some dear people are choosing to do the latter.

In his book *Beat the Blues before They Beat You*, Robert Leahy writes that the single most important issue to address for someone who is depressed is a feeling of hopelessness. "If you are absolutely convinced that life is hopeless, then you won't do anything to help yourself," he says. How may one hope if one has no hope? For some of us, medication or therapy or a combination of the two takes the edge off despair so that we can start hoping for hope again and become open to a transformation of ourselves and our unfulfilled desires.

The phrase "hoping for hope" leads us to a theological question about the virtue. That is, is *hope* a noun to receive or a verb to practice? Bangla, my mother tongue, turns the noun (*asha*) into a verb by adding the word *make* or *do* before it: *asha kohree*. Spanish has two words for it: *esperanza* is the noun and *esparar* the verb. In English, there's only one word for both the noun and verb forms, which leaves us in a quandary. "Hope is the thing with feathers, that perches in the soul," wrote the poet Emily Dickinson, transforming it into a mysterious, singing noun that doesn't require anything of the human heart.

But if hope is purely a gift, how do we grow in it as a virtue? A friend uses the metaphor of water in a well; the drawing of it takes effort, but the source is infused by unseen springs. Once we have a measure of it, we are able to draw from that well when thirsty. We can, to paraphrase the lines Emily Webster memorizes from William Shakespeare's *Love's Labour's Lost*, "muster our wits and stand in our own defense."

TIMELESS DEFENSES

Let's consider Emily's example to receive and practice a transforming hope that is infused by and centered on God. First, she tunes into hopeful *words* from her community. In the throes of depression, she's resistant to her grandfather's suggestion that they read *The Talisman*, a classic novel from the past by Sir Walter Scott. She doesn't want to read it; she wants contemporary nonfiction assigned by the college professors teaching sociology to her friends. Stacks of library books consumed in solitude don't suffice because she can't explore their themes and debate their literary merit in community with other readers.

Discussing poetry and politics was one of the things that drew her to Don. In an argument with him about poetry, she quotes a few lines from *The Marshes of Glynn*, a poem by Sidney Lanier, that foreshadow how she will build her own nest:

As the marsh-hen secretly builds on the watery sod,
Behold I will build me a nest on the greatness of God:
I will fly in the greatness of God as the marsh-hen
flies . . .

One Sunday in church, Reverend Macdonald quotes the bracing Shakespearean lines, and Emily takes them as her mantra. Later that night, as she's mulling them over, an idea leaps into her mind. She decides to form a group to study the poet Robert Browning under Miss Fowler, her high school English teacher. After their community discussion of Browning's poem "David Singing before Saul," which she'd first read in a book given to her by Don, a few stanzas bolster Emily as she crosses the slough on a windy winter's night:

> How good is man's life, the mere living! how fit to employ
> All the heart and the soul and the senses forever in joy.

I read this poem in its entirety for the first time after seeing these verses quoted by Auntie Maud, and revisited the biblical scene (Samuel 16:14–23) when a shepherd boy calms the King of Israel with music. Browning describes how David's artistry offered hope to Saul's true self, which is probably why the poem inspired and uplifted Emily. She wonders how Don might understand it: "Don hasn't the joy in life, and the faith in people, and the—the love of God that Browning has." In her view, Browning's reflections on the battle between right and wrong ("I count life just a stuff / To try the soul's strength on . . .") are a tonic, as is learning from the book's introduction that the poet's schooling was irregular but that his true education was "a long life time of eager, wide, and absorptive culture until death itself."

Emily also replaces voices that pull her down—Don's and Annette's, particularly—with voices of encouragement. She listens eagerly to Cab's story of giving up college to provide for his family, Betsy's description of a year in California during which she reconnected with herself, and even hopeful examples from her own past—her mother, who endured tragedies but never lost her zeal to speak out on behalf of others, and her grandmother, teaching school inside her small home when there were no other alternatives.

Emily draws hope, too, from another kind of poetry—the carols and hymns of faith she sings for her grandfather: "Carols were like no other songs, she thought. They sounded so pure and sweet, as though they came from heaven." Like David before King Saul in Browning's poem, and like Emily, we can sing songs that resound with praise to God.

Many authors from the past who wrote poems, stories, and songs of hope filled their well by meditating on the Bible. The Old and New Testaments are a rich source of hope, reassuring us again and again that God loves us and is tenderly caring for us, even in the midst of despair. In the King James translation, the word *hope* shows up 130 times in 121 different verses.

Saint Paul spells out how the muscle of hope grows stronger in seasons of despair: "Not only that, but we rejoice in our sufferings, knowing that suffering produces endurance, and endurance produces character, and character produces hope" (Romans 5:3–4 ESV). A sign of this production of hope is giving thanks to a God of love. At church, while the minister prays, a newly hopeful Emily says her own prayer of gratitude.

Second, Emily spends time with hopeful *role models*, particularly her erstwhile English teacher Miss Fowler and her piano teacher Miss Cobb, characters who also show up in the Betsy-Tacy books. Auntie Maud takes quite a bit of time in this novel to describe the beauty of Miss Cobb's character. All of Deep Valley knows that she broke off her engagement to raise her dead sister's four children, three of whom eventually also died of tuberculosis. Miss Cobb is consistently cheerful and has a rewarding life even though she set aside a desire for marriage out of duty, and Emily reflects on the older woman's ability to practice hope even in the most trying of circumstances.

When Miss Fowler shares why she recommends a particular biography of Abraham Lincoln, *The True Story of a Great Life* by William H. Herndon, she tries to encourage Emily with a sustaining philosophy: "You've discovered, I see, that we have to build our lives out of what material we have. It's as though we were given a heap of blocks and told to build a house." Miss Fowler's small apartment is full of books, magazines, and paintings, echoing Browning's pursuit of and Emily's hunger for culture and education. The apartment is a space that seems narrow on the outside but is wide and deep from the inside, akin to Miss Fowler's life. In this mentor's dwelling place, Emily meets Jed Wakeman, a young man who shares her desire to get to know the Syrian community of newly arrived immigrants in their town. Jed sees Emily with eyes of acceptance and love. Unlike Don. When he and Emily become a couple, Miss Fowler's "black eyes [have] the matchmaker's sparkle."

Third, Emily practices hopeful *service*, putting her talents to use for the sake of newcomers, immigrants who are over-looked and ostracized by fictional Deep Valley residents. In real life, a Syrian community existed in Mankato, Minnesota, Auntie Maud's hometown, as described by Jia Tolentino in the *New Yorker*:

> From 1899 to 1919, the arrival of nearly ninety thousand Syrian immigrants was recorded. In 1924, Philip Hitti, a Lebanese-American professor and pioneer of Arabic studies, estimated that there were around two hundred thousand Syrian immigrants living in the U.S. by 1920. There was, in fact, a "Little Syria" in Mankato, where Marguerite Marsh—Lovelace's inspiration for Emily Webster—lived with her grandfather and worked with the immigrant com-munity instead of going away to school. Marsh, whose brother, parents, and grandmother all died before she turned fourteen, served with the Y.M.C.A. during the First World War, working in a canteen in France.

"In many ways, that book told a true story," Lovelace wrote to a friend, about "Emily of Deep Valley," in 1973.

Syrian characters are the "other" in Auntie Maud's story, but she handles them in an exemplary way. Instead of encountering bias in the "bones of the book," as we discussed in the chapter about *Anne of Green Gables*, we see particular, fully fleshed Syrian characters through the eyes of hospitable Emily and her grandfather.

Persecuted in their home country for religious beliefs, these families are struggling to make a living and become part of the Deep Valley community. For twenty years, the townspeople—secondary characters whose biases are clearly wrong—have kept them at a distance. But Auntie Maud doesn't allow us to do that in her writing. She introduces us to the feisty, outgoing Kalil and his stout compatriot Yusef, and we smile at the closeness of their friendship. She has Kalil remove his cap and say, "Goodbye, my grandpa. I am full of thanks to you. Peace to your age," and our hearts melt. We celebrate Christmas with the shining-eyed Syrian children and visit them at Easter, imagining the taste of *kahik*, a sweet cake, and watching their traditional egg-breaking contest. Still, the townspeople in the story aren't convinced and even use a derogatory term when talking about the Syrians: "dago."

READING *EMILY OF DEEP VALLEY* WITH CHILDREN

Racial slurs in classic books can lead to talk about expulsion from the canon. But a discerning reader will see that it matters *who says the slur* and *how other characters respond to it*. When reading this book aloud to children, I find Bobby Sibley's use of "dago" as a negative slang word a good place to stop and discuss the danger of such ignorant labels. At one point in the book, Emily turns to Bobby, one of the Deep Valley boys she is trying to recruit to join a club, to ask if he knows any Syrian boys: "'Naw! They're . . .' he stopped, and looked cautiously at his father."

I'd pause there for a moment. "Why does Bobby stop and look at his father?" I might ask a circle of upturned faces gathered around me. "What is he about to say, do you think?" I'd listen to their answers and talk about their predictions, and then we'd keep reading:

"What were you going to say, son?"
"You told me not to say it."
"Then I'm glad you didn't."

I'd pause again. "Have your parents ever warned you not to use certain words when it comes to talking about other people?" I'd ask, and we'd talk about that for a bit. I might introduce the term *slur*. "Have you ever been called something like that? How did it make you feel?"

Then I'd keep reading: "'They're not dagos, are they, Dad?' asked Bobby, and grinned broadly to have outwitted his parent."

"What does this encounter tell you about Bobby?" I'd ask, and we'd discuss that. "Let's keep reading and see if his view of Kalil changes." (Spoiler: Bobby does go on to change, and by the end of the book, we find him visiting Kalil's home in the Syrian enclave to eat baklava as good friends do.)

As I kept reading, whether with a monocultural group or a diverse group of children, we'd probably discuss why Emily wants to "Americanize" the Syrians by teaching them English and how to become a citizen. Do the listening children think this is a good idea? Why or why not? I'd also want to talk about Bobby calling Kalil "Charley." We'd notice together that the narrator always calls the Syrian character Kalil, even when Bobby begins calling him "Charley." When do nick-names unite and when do they separate?

Imagine, though, that I'm an adult reading the book in a North American school where Syrian refugee children have been resettled. Read through the paragraphs I quoted earlier and picture a listening circle that includes brown children wearing headscarves. I doubt that Auntie Maud pictured her reading audience as Syrian children when she wrote the book; so how does her portrayal hold up without an educator to moderate and prompt reflection? You might disagree with this, but in my eyes, even without adult mediation, an astute child reader can see from the book that slurs separate us and are used only by ignorant people.

I admire how the author introduces the "other" in a way that brings us closer to the Syrians. Kalil, Yusuf, and Layla are not in the novel to serve as foils for Emily; we know them each intimately by the end of the story. And Emily is no outside savior figure; in fact, the children are more instrumental in her transformation than she in theirs. Bit by bit, the book illuminates how a growing affection for the Syrians and a desire to see them integrated into the community emancipates Emily from despair. That's why I think Syrian children today would feel empowered and celebrated by Auntie Maud's novel.

RENEWED IN HOPE

The author deftly uses place in the story to mirror Emily's transformation. As we noted earlier, Deep Valley's slough in winter provides the perfect metaphor of a desolate, apparently lifeless situation. But it's this "slough of Despond" (as John Bunyan described a season of despair in *Pilgrim's Progress*) that first brings Kalil and Yusef to Emily with their basket of frogs' legs. By the last chapter, the slough in late May is full of sweet-smelling purple and white flowers and birds singing in trees with new leaves. Beyond it, Emily can see the ever-present humble rooftops of the Syrians *and* the lights of the town. She is renewed in hope, thanks to hopeful words, mentors, and a practice of service to the "alien and stranger," a category of people close to God's heart (see Leviticus 19:33–34).

This connection between hospitality to the "other" and a renewal of hope makes *Emily of Deep Valley* my favorite of Auntie Maud's stories. As a young reader, I saw myself mirrored in Emily, as we all do. But I was also Yusef, Kalil, and Layla, longing for a warm American welcome. I wanted "Deep Valley" to give *me* a cup of hot cocoa, a unanimous vote, a joyful Babel of hurrahs, a hearty handshake, a bottle of violet perfume. I wanted American neighbors to come to *our* house so my father could overflow with hospitality: "What a blessed day! You have come to my house! It is yours."

These days, when I reread this story, I picture another young newcomer to America steeping her soul in *Emily of Deep Valley*. I can see her now, turning the pages, as enraptured as I was, with dimples as deep as Layla's in both cheeks. She will imagine herself as Emily; she will see herself as Layla. I pray that she'll grow up to be both a receiver and a giver of hope.

REFLECT AND DISCUSS

1. Poetry offers solace in an individual or collective dark night of the soul. Find and share a particular poem that fills you with hope.

2. Pay attention to your emotions after you spend time on the internet. Are there sources of news that lead you to feel low? Do you follow people on social media who build your hope? How might you turn up the volume on voices of hope and tune out voices that bring you down?

3. How are you welcoming the "alien and stranger" (see Leviticus 19:33–34) in your community?

4. Emily's friendship with her English teacher inspires us to seek closer relationships with elders who live hopefully despite adversity. Do you have such a friendship? If not, how might you seek one out?

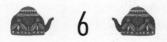

6

PUSILLANIMITY AND COURAGE

THE HOBBIT BY J. R. R. TOLKIEN

There is more in you of good than you know, child of the kindly West. Some courage and some wisdom, blended in measure. If more of us valued food and cheer and song above hoarded gold, it would be a merrier world.

—Thorin

Many aficionados of Middle Earth—the magical realm created by J. R. R. Tolkien, or Uncle John Ronald, as his nephews in real life called him—prefer *The Lord of the Rings* trilogy over *The Hobbit*. The trilogy has deeper themes and a more complicated plot than *The Hobbit* does. It even features a few secondary female characters, unlike *The Hobbit*. But for me as a young adult decades ago, it was a gift to encounter Bilbo Baggins as the main character of a story. I could easily cheer for this engaging, earthy, perpetually hungry hobbit, the name Uncle John Ronald coined for mythical creatures dwelling in a peaceful land called "The Shire." I was about to make crucial life decisions, and I needed a hero who could inspire me to be courageous. As a seasoned reader by the time I was a teenager, it was easy to imagine myself as any protagonist; I didn't need the mirror of gender to see myself in Bilbo. He has more foibles than Frodo, the protagonist of *The Lord of the Rings*. With a love for comfort and safety and a tendency toward complaining and conniving, Bilbo was me. He still is. Perhaps he's you too.

Before we explore the courage Bilbo demonstrates in *The Hobbit*, I'd like to have a robust imaginary conversation with Uncle John Ronald about adoption, race, and culture.

FANTASTIC FIASCO

First, I'd want to talk about how so many novels feature adoptees, but few explore the grief and trauma of adoption. Take Frodo, the hero of the *Lord of the Rings* trilogy, who is raised in the Brandybuck clan on his mother's side for nine years before being adopted by his paternal cousin

Bilbo. We're told briefly that Frodo lost both parents when he was twelve in a nighttime boating accident. Wouldn't he remember their drowning at different points through his hero's journey? Why did they both go outside at night in a boat, leaving their only son behind? Why doesn't he seek to learn more about them?

Second, I'd like to ask Uncle John Ronald how views of race and culture in the real world find their way into an imaginary world. For example, when describing dwarves, hobbits, dragons, witches, goblins, orcs, and elves, a writer might be tempted to use "species-wide" character descriptions. In the Harry Potter series, for example, *all* goblins are shrewd, swarthy, and calculating. In the Narnia books, *all* marshwiggles have a dour view of life—and we'll talk about "the Calormene problem" when we get to *The Silver Chair* in chapter 9. These "people-wide" generalizations about characters in fantasy novels echo stereotypes affiliated with different ethnic groups in our own world—like a customer service worker who eyes me dubiously as I approach, and instantly I assume she's thinking *all* immigrants from South Asia want to haggle over prices.

But let's confront the particulars in Uncle John Ronald's books. In Middle Earth, Gollum the villain descends from the darker-skinned branch of hobbits; Frodo, the hero, has fairer-skinned ancestors. When a slain Haradrim warrior crashes at Sam's feet, we learn that the enemy has brown skin and black plaits of hair braided with gold. The people of Far Harad are described as "black men like half-trolls with white eyes and red tongues" and "troll-men." Throughout the trilogy, good elves are tall and fair, and evil orcs are dark-skinned and squint-eyed. A letter describes the author's vision of these irredeemable creatures as "squat, broad, flat-nosed, sallow-skinned, with wide mouths and slant eyes; in fact degraded and repulsive versions of the (to Europeans) least lovely Mongol-types."

At least Uncle John Ronald modified his intentions a bit by adding "to Europeans"; still, as a teen reader, I flinched at the Asian descriptions of evil characters in *The Lord of the Rings*. Erstwhile fan Christina Warmbrunn writes poignantly about how she sees Blackness represented in Middle Earth:

> In *The Return of the King* . . . there is a harrowing sequence where the halflings Frodo and Sam pretend to be Orcs to sneak past Sauron's army:
>
> > Presently two orcs came into view. One was clad in ragged brown and was armed with a bow of horn; it was of a small breed, black-skinned, with wide and snuffling nostrils: evidently a tracker of some kind (Ch. 2, "The Land of Shadow").
>
> This passage not only codes Orcs as Black, it uses specific descriptors ("wide and snuffling nostrils") that echo Jim Crow-era caricatures. The use of the pronoun

"it," as well as the animalistic vocabulary ("breed," "tracker") echoes white supremacist ideologies of purity that differentiate Black people as a separate, explicitly subhuman, species.

And then there's the Jewishness of the dwarves. When we meet the dwarves in *The Hobbit*, they are a group with shared negative attributes, "calculating folk with a great idea of the value of money; some are tricky and treacherous and pretty bad lots." More than three decades after publishing the book, the author spoke about the Jewish-Dwarvish connection. "I didn't intend it, but when you've got these people on your hands, you've got to make them different, haven't you?" he said during a 1964 BBC interview. "The dwarves of course are quite obviously, wouldn't you say that in many ways they remind you of the Jews? Their words are Semitic, obviously, constructed to be Semitic. The hobbits are just rustic English people."

During the Second World War, however, in a drafted letter, he clarified his position on the Jewish people to a Nazi-sympathizing German publisher who asked about his racial ancestry. "Thank you for your letter," Uncle John Ronald wrote. "I regret that I am not clear as to what you intend by *arisch* [Aryan]. I am not of Aryan extraction: that is Indo-Iranian; as far as I am aware none of my ancestors spoke Hindustani, Persian, Gypsy, or any related dialects. But if I am to understand that you are enquiring whether I am of Jewish origin, I can only reply that I regret that I appear to have no ancestors of that gifted people."

Another regret he had was over the treatment of Black people in his native South Africa, which he described as "horrifying" in a letter to his son. I wonder how he might have reacted to Christina Warmbrunn's sorrow if he could have met her face-to-face at the end of his life, when his oldest grandchild was about her age. Would he have expressed deep regret about the ways he employed race in his books? Would he have admitted to their harmful flaws?

We might be able to imagine such a change taking place in Uncle John Ronald over the course of his life. Even Gandalf evolves from the start of *The Hobbit*, where he "never minded explaining his cleverness more than once," to his last appearance in *Unfinished Tales: The Lost Lore of Middle-Earth*. "Merry he could be," Uncle John Ronald wrote, "and kindly to the young and simple, and yet quick at times to sharp speech and the rebuking of folly; but he was not proud, and sought neither power nor praise, and thus far and wide he was beloved among all those that were not themselves proud."

BILBO THE HERO

One of the "simple" characters who saw Gandalf clearly was Bilbo Baggins. To this day, a closer look at Bilbo's hero's journey encourages me to choose magnanimity over pusillanimity. (Now there's a pair of words we don't use in everyday conversation.) According to Thomas Aquinas, *magnanimity* (from Latin *magnus*, "great," and *animus*, "soul") is a "stretching forth of the mind to great things." We are magnanimous when we desire and attempt great things. Pusillanimity (from Latin *pusillus*, "very small," and *animus*, "soul"), on the other hand, is a smallness of soul that shrinks from noble or arduous tasks. This vice, which stems from fear, is kept in check by the virtue of courage.

A hero must resist pusillanimity to embark on a journey. Joseph Campbell, an American mythologist and writer, noticed storytelling patterns throughout the world that followed the same narrative arc. In his book *The Hero with a Thousand Faces*, Campbell described the three stages of a monomyth, or heroic journey: departure (sets out on an adventure to an unknown world, willingly or unwillingly), initiation (goes through trials, meets friends, conquers foes), and return (in some sense to the place of embarkation, albeit changed and victorious). This commonality in story structure across cultures and throughout time reflects an innate human desire for a life of purpose.

Maybe I, like Bilbo, was designed to be the protagonist of a page-turner.

DEPARTURE

A call to adventure in a monomyth is an invitation to change; these show up in our lives as well. For us, living an epic story may look a lot different than moving through traditional "greeting-card-moment" life passages such as getting married, becoming a parent, moving to a new town, starting a job, or becoming a grandparent. Instead, it's usually precipitated by an *uncommon* event that upends stability. Disruption from the common life might be personal—getting fired from a job, caring for an aging parent, raising a child with a disability, confronting an addiction, losing a spouse, or being diagnosed with a disease. Or the call may come in the midst of societal chaos like war, disasters, epidemics, or injustice. In all of these cases, our souls, like Bilbo's, are given the choice to widen in magnanimity or shrink back in pusillanimity.

For my husband and me, one such chaotic situation came in our twenties with a diagnosis of infertility that left us without medical options. This closed door freed us to accept a job in India. There, an orphanage invited us to adopt twin babies who had been born prematurely. If that wasn't a call to adventure, I'm not sure what is. From time to time, we have grieved the loss of a "normal" way of becoming parents, but as the years pass, it's clear this journey has taken us to life-giving places and relationships we never would have discovered otherwise. Mothering another woman's sons has brought about profound, beautiful changes in my life. I think of their first mother often and pray for her journey.

Our sons, who weren't given a choice as babies, were forced into the uncommon life of being raised by people unrelated to them biologically. Their narrative now as adults is to live courageously and seek healing after the trauma of abandonment and the displacement of adoption. As in most heroes' journeys, meaningful victories and contributions will come *because* of that wound, not in spite of it. But they need courage to step into the arena.

When a "non-greeting-card" moment arrives in our lives, minimizing the pain isn't a solution because there are no guarantees that more pain won't come. It undoubtedly will. That's why it's tempting to escape into addiction or pursue distraction. But frankly—and I say this as a person who struggles to muster courage—those are pusillanimous attempts to numb pain. The best way forward is to deploy the virtue. The dictionary defines courage as "the ability to do something that frightens one." Nelson Mandela elaborated on this from his own experience of incarceration in South Africa: "I learned that courage was not the absence of fear, but the triumph over it. The brave man is not he who does not feel afraid, but he who conquers that fear."

How might we gather the courage to face what's ahead?

Bilbo's story sheds light on how to defeat fear. Bit by bit, Bilbo resists pusillanimity, builds courage, and achieves his quest. His call to adventure comes from Gandalf, a wizard who chooses him to help the dwarves reclaim their home. Bilbo's two lines of ancestry are initially at war with each other. At first, his Baggins side resists this call. He wants to remain in his cozy home in the Shire, where he can retain respectability, safety, routine, and his comfortable, luxurious habits. Isn't this our motivation, too, when it comes to the possibility of our lives being turned upside down?

However, Bilbo's Tookish side—the part that loves maps, fireworks, smoke rings, elves, runes, letters, songs, and stories—is intrigued. As the dwarves' deep-throated singing accompanies a beautiful golden harp, the music is so entrancing, Bilbo forgets everything but the dwarves' craftsmanship and desire for beautiful things. The Tookish part of his nature suddenly desires to explore the great mountains far away from the Shire. When he overhears talk about slaying a dragon and the possibility of not returning from the quest, the Baggins part of him regains the upper hand. Even as Bilbo quails and dissolves into a shrieking heap of fear, Gandalf affirms Bilbo's potential to the dwarves, describing him as one of the best in the world when it comes to burgling and comparing his courage to that of a dragon's.

Like Bilbo, those of us with the tendency to shrink from adventure don't believe we're capable of greatness. We know our own flaws, fears, and failures too well, and many of us battle what has been called impostor syndrome. First described by psychologists Suzanne Imes and Pauline Rose Clance in 1978, this internal condition occurs when we are unable to internalize and accept success. We attribute our accomplishments to luck rather than ability, and we fear that others will eventually unmask us as frauds. This makes it difficult to push through resistance. "Why would someone like *me* be able to persevere through this trial to emerge a hero?" we ask ourselves. "It's clearly time for my luck to run out and for people to see through my act." At the start of his story, Bilbo demonstrates a kind of impostor syndrome. It is Gandalf who believes in his capacity for integrity, loyalty, and leadership. We, too, need powerful eyes to see our better selves; a divine confidence in our capacity builds the courage to persevere through obstacles.

A caveat: sometimes heroic behavior actually *is* a facade for pride. Seeking approval from others, we impersonate a courageous person without actually becoming one. Pride stirs in Bilbo after he overhears a dwarf's derisive comment—that Gandalf's "burglar" is more like a grocer—and moves our hero to turn the handle of the door and enter the room. In the moment, the Tookish side of him would give up even feasting and comfort to be perceived by the dwarves as fierce. Pride, however, isn't enough motivation to actually embark on his journey: as the night deepens, the Baggins side regains the upper hand. After oversleeping and waking to an empty house, part of Bilbo is relieved that the others have departed without him, and yet he's also somewhat disappointed, a response that surprises him.

That's probably why, when Gandalf reappears and issues a command, Bilbo leaves his beloved hobbit hole without a backward look or even a handkerchief. "Off you go!" says Gandalf, and Bilbo obeys. "Sometimes the bravest and most important thing you can do is just show up," says author Brené Brown. Bilbo does exactly that, running as fast as he can down the lane to show up for his appointment with the dwarves.

INITIATION

Once the call to adventure is accepted, heroes enter the second and longest part of a journey, described as "initiation" by Joseph Campbell. This includes training by a mentor, honing talents, and acquiring tools through a series of tests and trials.

TRAINING BY A MENTOR. Gandalf never wavers in his decision to choose Bilbo for this quest. If "perfect love casts out fear," as Jesus's disciple John said in 1 John 4:18 (NASB1995), then the confidence of a Great Someone who knows us better than we know ourselves fortifies our courage. It's even more heartening when that Someone journeys with us to mentor us. At times, that mentor is apparent to us, and we sense intimate companionship; in other seasons, the Presence is unseen, and we feel deserted and alone. This is what Gandalf does for Bilbo, beginning to train his "burglar" shortly after he selects him.

Catching sight of three trolls, Bilbo is frightened and disgusted. He wishes desperately to avoid a confrontation, but once again, the Tookish part of him wants to impress the dwarves. In a foolish effort to win his companions' approval, and also because he has read many adventure stories, Bilbo tries to pick the trolls' pockets. His burgling doesn't work, and the dwarves are captured.

When Gandalf comes to the rescue, the wizard employs a skill to defeat the trolls that is within Bilbo's reach—staying hidden and using words to trick them into fighting. Bilbo watches, listens, and learns from this strategy of using secrecy and cleverness instead of force. While the wizard could have wielded fire and light, powers not accessible to his mentee, Gandalf models instead a strategy that even someone as relatively powerless as a hobbit might use in the future. In time, Bilbo does just that, hiding and throwing out insults to enrage a troop of spiders until they lose control of themselves and are defeated.

Gandalf again does this sort of within-reach mentoring when he engages with Beorn, a Man-Bear hybrid and fierce territorial governor. The wizard takes Bilbo in with him first and then brings in the dwarves intermittently in twos and threes instead of in one large group. The hobbit learns Gandalf's way of getting what he wants—welcome and shelter for their entire company—by distracting a threatening listener with fascinating conversation. As pairs or trios of dwarves join them, Beorn waves aside the interruptions thanks to Gandalf's engaging storytelling. The wizard stretches out his tale so that Beorn almost inadvertently becomes host to a large group of unwanted guests. In turn, when the time comes for Bilbo to change the behavior of an untamable creature, he uses clever conversation to get what he needs from Smaug the dragon.

Gandalf's mentoring is akin to that of Jesus's discipling of Peter, James, and John: taking those being formed into interactions with others to equip them for a future without his physical presence. Halfway through *The Hobbit*, when Gandalf announces his departure, Bilbo weeps because he had hoped Gandalf would always be present to rescue and guide them. But as with Jesus's friends, a mentor's departure is often necessary for heroes in training to accomplish great things. Hinting, perhaps, at the Holy Spirit, Uncle John Ronald has Gandalf show up again and again in Bilbo's story—albeit unexpectedly and often hidden—bringing comfort, company, and courage with each appearance.

HONING TALENTS. In a hero's journey, power is often "made perfect in weakness," as the apostle Paul wrote (2 Corinthians 12:9). Traits that might be labeled as liabilities in other scenarios strangely become useful in an adventure to which we are particularly called. For other work, we are disqualified for being too old or young, brown or white, male or female, quiet or talkative, outgoing or shy—and the list goes on. Maybe, like Bilbo, we are too small of stature, which one might think disqualifies a person from being a hero. But that theory turns out to be untrue.

As Bilbo heads off to spy on the trolls, his movement through the woods is silent and unnoticeable. He realizes that his hobbit's ability to move quietly is a talent not shared by the dwarves and sure to come in handy on this quest. Throughout the story, this ability comes into play: when Bilbo is in hiding within the elves' domain, when the spiders neither hear nor see his coming, and as he keeps out of reach of goblins and Gollum. It's something larger and louder people couldn't do even if they had a magic ring. The wonder of this particular skill is that it stems from Bilbo's small size, a trait usually associated with weakness.

Another talent he has is in games. He puts his riddling capacity to good use in his encounters with Gollum and Smaug. A skill in aiming and throwing enables him to defeat a horde of vicious enemies—spiders attacking him and his friends. In the nick of time, Bilbo hurls a stone with perfect accuracy. It smashes into the spider's head, and the creature drops to the ground, immobilized. Bilbo's next throw snaps into a web and kills another spider. He keeps aiming and throwing with great accuracy—as he learned in the games he played as a child—until the spiders flee in defeat.

Stone-throwing by a hero who was overlooked because of size is also in the Old Testament, when David takes off his heavy borrowed armor, wields a simple skill he has honed through the years, and takes down a giant. So-called small capacities, developed through practice, are underestimated in battle but may be put to mighty use.

A third, useful talent of Bilbo's is to enjoy simple pleasures not valued in the marketplace. When Thorin, driven by a love of wealth, refuses to parley with men and elves who are playing harps and warming the cold air with sweet music, Bilbo wants desperately to leave the dark, cold mountain and join the joking and feasting by the warm fire. Suffering instead through a long and hungry winter in darkness for the sake of keeping more treasure? That seems like a waste to Bilbo, and rightfully so. His love of everyday pleasures motivates him to make the right choice: to give away the Arkenstone.

ACQUIRING TOOLS. Through the initiation stage of a journey, a hero acquires tools. In the trolls' cave, Bilbo picks up a small sword that will be put to great use in both *The Hobbit* and *The Lord of the Rings* trilogy. He first glimpses its power when lost in a dark place where goblins are running amok. As the blade glows in the dark, he remembers goblin wars that had been won throughout history, and his resolve is bolstered.

Next, he uses the sword to accomplish something that magnifies his heart with courage: single-handedly slaying another ferocious spider. A story's midpoint is a key component of story structure, and Bilbo's battle with this spider is a perfect example. Producer John Yorke defines a midpoint as "the moment when each protagonist embraces for the first time the quality they will need to become complete and finish their story. It's when they discover a truth about themselves." In this crucial scene, after Bilbo uses Sting to kill the spider, he falls unconscious. Then comes the midpoint, after which Bilbo is metaphorically "born again" to become a bold leader. He wakes from a deep sleep to find the dead spider beside him and discovers that the blade of his sword is black. Killing the spider alone in the dark without help makes Bilbo feel as if he's changed completely, becoming a new person with boldness and force. He wipes his sword clean, names it Sting, and strides away.

A tool isn't salvific in and of itself; it's what the hero accomplishes with it that matters. In the same dark cavern where he first wielded Sting, Bilbo finds his second talisman: a magic ring that makes the wearer invisible. As you know if you've read the trilogy, this powerful piece of jewelry will also play a central role in *The Lord of the Rings*. Next, Thorin gives Bilbo a coat of mithril, which we later discover is worth more than all the land in the Shire and everything in it. The coat also proves to be helpful to Bilbo's heir, Frodo, saving Frodo's life in the thick of battle. In fact, many of the tools that Bilbo picks up in *The Hobbit* are more central to the success of the next generation than to Bilbo himself. Whether we are magnanimous or pusillanimous with the treasures we acquire along the journey shapes not only us but the future.

The fourth and final treasure that Bilbo picks up is the beautiful, mystical Arkenstone, called the "Heart of the Mountain." His resistance to the enchantment of this prized jewel is the key to achieving his quest, as he must muster the courage both to find it and then to give it up. This precedent—relinquishing a prize beyond measure—is a precursor of Bilbo's brave and difficult choice to pass his beloved ring on to Frodo in *The Fellowship of the Ring*. He resists the shrinking of his soul into a Gollum-esque condition.

Practicing courage in every situation, big or small, is the best way to gain more of it. Sitting back in a dentist's chair, calling a politician's office, boarding a flight, entering a room of strangers, declaring our love, joining a protest, holding our tongue: courage looks different for each of us, and a new day brings new chances to develop it. Bilbo must enter Smaug's cave three times before he picks up the Arkenstone, and the first time is the hardest. Every trial that Bilbo endures makes him progressively bolder. By the end of the story, he has transformed into the hero and warrior that Gandalf initially told the dwarves he had tried in vain to find—great-souled and brave, addressed as "Bilbo the Magnificent" by the Elvenking.

COURAGE FROM THE INSIDE

But courageous actions aren't enough on their own; courageous motivations are needed also. Bilbo's heroic journey has an inward as well as an external arc. As his actions grow bolder, his intentions become nobler.

In his confrontation with Gollum, Bilbo makes a courageous choice driven by neither fear nor pride. He is moved instead by pity, opting not to stab and kill a defenseless opponent but to escape instead. The presence of such compassion fuels courage; the lack of it is linked to pusillanimity. Pope Francis made this clear when discussing why people are reluctant to visit prisoners. "They think, 'It's dangerous! They are bad people,'" the pope said about our fear. "Each one of us is capable of doing the same thing done by that man or woman in jail. All of us are capable of sinning and making the same mistake in life. They are not worse than you and I."

Bilbo's compassion likely stems from the connection he has made by playing a game of riddles with Gollum, a pastime common to both from childhood. Hobbits know that the riddle game is so old and sacred that even evil creatures don't like to cheat when playing it. Uncle John Ronald stirs pity in the reader's heart by taking us into Gollum's mind during this scene: "Riddles were . . . the only game he had ever played with other funny creatures sitting in their holes in the long, long ago, before he lost all his friends . . . when he lived with his grandmother in a hole in a bank by a river." It's almost as if compassion for this miserable opponent creates space in Bilbo's soul, because he's filled with a new strength that allows him to leap over Gollum's head.

If compassion generates courage in Bilbo's soul, so does loyalty, which starts to stir in him soon after his escape from Gollum and the goblins. He wanders down the mountain and through a valley, but soon a disconcerting thought begins to plague him: Should he go back into the dark tunnels to search for his friends? After some rumination, he decides that doing so is his duty and reunites with his friends. Loyalty also leads him to accompany the dwarves into the elves' prison and helps him make up his mind at the last minute not to desert them. Bilbo stays true to his friends despite their fickle feelings toward him. Sometimes the dwarves grumble at and blame him, at other times they laud and thank him, but Bilbo always keeps his end of the bargain.

Eventually, this admirable quality of tenacity in friendship leads Bilbo to alienate his friends in order to save them. Consumed with greed over treasure, Thorin refuses to pay anything to those who killed the dragon at great cost to themselves and damage to their town. When Bilbo gives up the beautiful Arkenstone in an effort to make peace, both the Elvenking and Bard, the leader of men, greet him with honor. Gandalf claps Bilbo on the back, reminding everyone present that his chosen burglar always exceeds expectations.

Bilbo does more than give up the Arkenstone—he risks his own life. When he confesses his deed to an enraged

Thorin, the King of the Dwarves almost tosses Bilbo over a cliff. In the nick of time, Gandalf manages to save "his Burglar." By the end, though, Mr. Baggins gains what he initially sought: the dwarves' gratitude and admiration. A repentant Thorin's last words are a testament to Bilbo's character and the gift of a "small" life that delights in friends and fire and feast: "There is more in you of good than you know, child of the kindly West. Some courage and some wisdom, blended in measure. If more of us valued food and cheer and song above hoarded gold, it would be a merrier world."

RETURN

Just before they cross the bridge back to Hobbiton, where the adventure started, even Gandalf is surprised by the change in Bilbo's character, declaring that he's not the same hobbit who left the Shire. The wizard is right: Bilbo has changed, but our hero has also become more of himself.

It soon becomes clear, however, that he has lost his reputation at home. Even though now he is a friend of elves, honored by dwarves, men, and wizards, in his own community, he is seen as strange and not respectable. Bilbo, however, no longer cares about the admiration of others. He spends the rest of his days in the Shire happily, writing poems and visiting the elves from time to time.

Uncle John Ronald ends the story by underlining one attribute that hasn't changed: Bilbo's humility. Gandalf affirms their friendship and the quality of his character but also reminds him of his rightful place as one small hobbit in an enormous world. Bilbo answers with a grateful laugh. He sees both the smallness *and* the usefulness of his true self—a realization that is perhaps the greatest victory of all.

A call to adventure like Bilbo's, typically in the guise of disruption and chaos, is bound to come in every person's life. No matter our circumstances, each of us can muster the courage to accept a divine invitation and embark on a moral journey. If we accept the call, we begin the slow, arduous process of transformation. Like Bilbo, we will make foolish mistakes, but the good news is that we will be mentored by someone who loves us as we muddle along. Through small and big tests, as we resist pusillanimity, our courage will blossom. "Life shrinks or expands in proportion to one's courage," wrote Anaïs Nin.

Hopefully, by the end of our journey, we will achieve something we never dreamed of when we took that first step. We will have become heroes, albeit unsung and unseen by most folk, much like Bilbo Baggins the Magnificent. Maybe that's why so many of us read and reread *The Hobbit*: we sense a call to adventure from God and long for the courage to respond to it.

REFLECT AND DISCUSS

1. Have you ever experienced—or are you experiencing now—unforeseen chaos or disruption in your own journey?
2. If this disruption was—or is—a call to adventure, what might accepting it look like?
3. Who believes in your capacity to endure and triumph throughout this difficult journey?
4. How are you uniquely equipped to be victorious? Who taught you well? What are some unique talents that might serve you? What tools and technologies, worldly or otherwise, are in your arsenal?
5. What are some small risks you might take to resist the human soul's tendency to shrink over time?

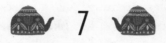

7
SELF-INDULGENCE AND TEMPERANCE

LITTLE WOMEN BY LOUISA MAY ALCOTT

For in that sad yet happy hour, she had learned not only
the bitterness of remorse and despair, but the sweetness
of self-denial and self-control.

—Louisa May Alcott

J o March remains one of the most beloved characters
in literature, particularly for women who are writers.
Nora and Delia Ephron, Barbara Kingsolver, Jhumpa Lahiri,
Jane Smiley, Anne Tyler, Mary Gordon, Stephenie Meyer,
Doris Lessing, Margaret Atwood, A. S. Byatt, and Simone

de Beauvoir all credit Louisa May Alcott (Aunt Louisa) for their aspirations. Ursula Le Guin said that Jo, whom she called "as close as a sister and as common as grass," made writing seem like something "even a girl could do."

When I first met Jo, I felt like she was me, a Bengali immigrant growing up in Flushing, Queens, in the body of a Concord, Massachusetts, nineteenth-century woman. She sought to be a professional writer in a culture that scorned women who sold art for money. And Jo succeeded, even though girls like her were supposed to write, draw, dance, act, and sing only for refinement, not for revenue. Where had I heard that before? In our middle-class Bengali family, a daughter's artistic talents were shown off only to impress prospective in-laws. As Aunt March reminded Jo's parents—and as it was for the three of us Bose daughters—marrying well was the top priority for girls of a certain class.

Jo also bucked the norms and constraints of femininity as defined by society. Running races; cutting off her hair; dressing simply; avoiding parties, fuss, and frills; taking solitary rambles; shoveling snow; befriending boys—these acts of rebellion seemed astounding to me. Revolutionary, even. Reading and rereading *Little Women* bolstered my own growing resistance to sexism. Best of all, she loved her three sisters and parents dearly. In an all-girl family like mine, Jo proved that daughters could be as valuable as sons. She took on the role I coveted—the sister with strong shoulders to lean on—and became the eventual provider of the March household, as did the author of the novel in real life.

AUNT LOUISA MAKES A LIVING

Little Women has been perceived as a feminist novel for generations. The author was bolder about interweaving her belief in women's suffrage into the novel, however, than she was about confronting racial injustice. When it comes to issues of race and culture in *Little Women*, we know the March family has sacrificed to fight for the Northern cause in the Civil War because it is "for the nation." But that's it. Asia, the faithful family servant, is neither explicitly described as Black nor given any backstory. She is a foil, present in the story solely to illuminate the characters we come to love in the novel. The German immigrant Hummel family, whose scarlet fever is (spoiler alert) the cause of beloved Beth's death, help the March girls and the readers of this novel learn how charity can cost the giver. They, too, are foils.

The interesting question is why Aunt Louisa didn't include more discussion of race in the novel, as she was an ardent abolitionist in real life. The dramatic and moralistic novel *Uncle Tom's Cabin*, published in 1852 by Harriet Beecher Stowe, another writer living in Concord, Massachusetts, undoubtedly influenced Aunt Louisa, who was twenty years old when it came out. She wrote *Little Women* fifteen years later, after her own father was forced to shut down one of his schools because he refused to expel a Black student. The Alcott family was part of the Underground Railroad, and when she was seven years old, Aunt Louisa opened an unused stove to discover a freedom seeker hiding inside. She taught him and others to read and write, and she served as a nurse in the Civil War so that she could contribute to ending slavery. Why, then, didn't she include more of her passionate abolitionist views in this novel? Aunt Louisa herself made the answer clear: she needed the book to sell. As a writer myself, I sympathize. There's pressure to meet readers' expectations, and at times our ideals and sales projections coexist in an uneasy tension.

MANIFESTO FOR A MUCH-NEEDED VIRTUE

When asked for his opinion of *Little Women*, G. K. Chesterton said he felt like "an intruder in that club of girls." A masculine reticence to read the book, however, might be more due to the title and publisher's marketing strategy than the story's deeper contents. One primary universal thread in Aunt Louisa's novel, for example, is that of spiritual formation. Meg, Jo, Beth, and Amy do their best to follow the path of self-denying Christian in John Bunyan's classic *Pilgrim's Progress*. I have yet to see this theme in any modern adaptation. At the heart, this story of four sisters—Chesterton's so-called club of girls—is a manifesto on a virtue desperately needed in our cultural moment: temperance.

Thomas Aquinas, co-opting Platonic thought, included temperance as one of four cardinal virtues, along with courage, justice, and prudence. This virtue, he wrote, modifies the most insatiable human passions: sex, drink, food, the desire for what one cannot achieve, anger, the desire to punish, and the desire to pursue vain curiosities. Under the umbrella of temperance, Aquinas included the self-denying practices of chastity, sobriety, abstinence, humility, meekness, clemency, and studiousness. To some extent, *Little Women* lauds all of these, and the March sisters demonstrate how the virtue of temperance is crucial in warding off an empty, squandered life.

TEMPERING OUR WAY TO THE GOOD LIFE

To most denizens of modern-day culture, temperance seems like an outdated joy killer. Self-denial in the pursuit of fame and fortune definitely isn't in vogue. As I scroll down the list of popular self-help titles, I see that we're called to a lot of things: "lean in," be "all in," "dare greatly," "dream big," be "untamed," "stop apologizing," and "think and grow rich." In our cultural moment, *Girl, Temper Yourself* wouldn't be the catchiest title for a book.

The problem is that chasing after luxury, desperately pursuing success, and expressing our emotions without self-denial results in a life marked by restlessness, envy, and discontent. As Brené Brown puts it, we live in a culture of "never enough" and have become "deeply steeped in comparison and fractured by disengagement." Maybe that's why a deep, slow steep in *Little Women* is a good way to resist some of our culture's most flagrant lies about self-indulgence—lies that shame, scold, and rob us of a truly good life.

Mrs. March, or "Marmee" as her daughters (and readers) call her, delivers lessons in temperance throughout *Little Women*, and the girls' relatable experiences teach them (and us) the benefits. In life as in the story, the author wholeheartedly believed in temperance, writing about her commitment in a letter to a friend: "[I] helped start a temperance society much needed in C[oncord]. I was secretary, and wrote records, letters, and sent pledges, etc." While she was a staunch activist in the restriction of alcohol—in her novel *Rose in Bloom*, for example, beloved Charlie dies of alcohol addiction—temperance with regard to other vain pursuits and desires is a theme throughout her fiction. In *Little Women*, we see that practicing temperance doesn't lead to a narrow life marked by sanctimony and legalism but instead to a wholesome life of love and peace.

TEMPERING CONSUMPTION

In the character of Meg, we see how and why to temper an unrestrained desire for wealth. A longing for luxuries leads the oldest March daughter into dangerous territory. In a quiet chapter toward the beginning of the book, the sisters and the young man who is their neighbor, Laurie, sit together in a shady nook and share their dreams about the future. "I should like a lovely house, full of all sorts of luxurious things—nice food, pretty clothes, handsome furniture, pleasant people, and heaps of money," Meg says. "I am to be mistress of it, and manage it as I like, with plenty of servants, so I never need work a bit." She believes that money is the way to attain her goal of a happy home. Soon, Meg sacrifices her true self at a party at the Moffats' house, letting a makeover in borrowed finery turn her into someone she is embarrassed about at home. As a young wife, Meg can't "help contrasting [Ned and Sallie Moffat's] fine house and carriage, many gifts, and splendid outfit, with her own, and secretly wishing she could have the same." She indulges in buying expensive silk cloth that she and John Brooke can't afford and then proceeds to hurt her beloved, hardworking husband by saying, "I'm tired of being poor."

Meg is quick to repent, however, and heed her mother's advice: "Money is a needful and precious thing,—and, when well used, a noble thing,—but I never want you to think it is the first or only prize to strive for. I'd rather see you poor men's wives, if you were happy, beloved, contented, than queens on thrones without self-respect and peace."

One of the best ways to displace money as life's first prize is through the practice of *generosity*; Marmee models that truth from the start of the novel. Although the girls are hesitant to give away their Christmas breakfast, they reap the reward of joy: "I think there were not in all the city four merrier people than the hungry little girls who gave away their breakfasts and contented themselves with bread and milk on Christmas morning," Aunt Louisa writes.

Marmee also teaches the girls the other secret to resisting the empty life of consumerism: the practice of *gratitude*. "When you feel discontented, think over your blessings, and be grateful," she says. This simple motto can make all the difference in exhausted, anxious, hurried lives and is backed up by science. Berkeley researchers recently discovered that expressing gratitude improves our well-being by shifting us away from toxic emotions and thoughts and may also have lasting positive effects on the brain. In *Little Women*, we see delightful results as Meg begins to be generous and grateful. Soon even Sallie Moffat prefers Meg's home to her own mansion; she looks about her "with wistful eyes, as if trying to discover the charm, that she might use it in her great house, full of splendid loneliness." Thanks to a tempering of consumption, Meg gains a truer, better version of her girlhood aspiration—a happy, hospitable home.

TEMPERING EMOTION

Jo helps us see how and why we should temper a tendency to be ruled by emotion. Emotional restraint is not exactly welcomed in our cultural context. Around us, on social media and in viral videos, we see anger, shame, despair, and bad moods erupting in bad behavior. But we still don't necessarily want to grow up and control ourselves. Perhaps that's why modern adaptations of *Little Women* celebrate a young Jo's impetuous spirit, passion, stubborn ways, and bold voice but play down her transformation into a self-disciplined adult. In the novel, however, Aunt Louisa makes it clear that emotions expressed without restraint result in disaster. Jo's anger almost causes Amy's death; irritation and grumpiness cost her a trip to Europe; and after Beth dies, despondency and despair spiral into a "moody, miserable state of mind."

These aren't emotions particular to the nineteenth century; they've been part of the human condition since the dawn of time. Previous generations tried to subdue them with harsh parental punishment, but that didn't work well either. Therapists make a living healing the damage done by the legalistic controlling of childhood emotions. These days, we're told to express our emotions fully—to blow off steam so it doesn't spew out in the wrong places. Some people book sessions in "rage rooms," where they can destroy plates with a baseball bat or bang dolls against a wall. Yet venting emotions doesn't seem to be lessening the fear, anger, and despair endemic in our era. Are we doomed to swing between emotional polar opposites from generation to generation—moving from severe, unhealthy suppression to childish, self-indulgent expression and back again? Not if we embrace the virtue of temperance, one of whose functions is to keep us from such extremes.

Jo eventually learns to govern her emotions thanks to her own remorse and two practices: self-control and prayer. Both are modeled by her mother, who teaches them to Jo first by "drawing the blowzy head to her shoulder and kissing the wet cheek so tenderly that Jo cried harder than ever." Marmee then confesses her own lifelong struggle to self-regulate, which gives an amazed Jo hope that denying oneself and turning to God for help can actually make a difference.

The good news in *Little Women* is that as Jo learns to govern her emotions, she doesn't turn into a dull, stiff, numb version of herself. In the last chapters of *Little Women*, after it's clear that Jo has attained maturity, Aunt Louisa tells us that "Jo never, never would learn to be proper," as our hero initiates a first kiss with "her Friedrich" and cries out her thanks to Marmee with the "loving impetuosity which she could never outgrow." In fact, Jo's sense of humor, love of fun, passionate nature, and ability to grieve and lament continue to mark her character until the end of *Jo's Boys*, the last of three novels about the March sisters. That's the gift of temperance: it develops in us a capacity to enjoy and express a full range of emotions without allowing them to rule us.

TEMPERING AMBITION

Both Amy and Jo show us how and why we should temper a desire for success. Although Amy's girlhood dream is to "be the best artist in the whole world," she comes to realize that talent isn't the same as genius. Marmee also offers wise words that seem apropos for those of us who humblebrag or promote our brands on social media. "There is not much danger that real talent or goodness will be overlooked long," she tells Amy. "Even if it is, the consciousness of possessing it and using it well should satisfy one, and the great charm of all power is modesty." *Modesty* is clearly Aunt Louisa's favorite synonym for *temperance*.

In the latter half of the book, we see a new ambition emerge in Amy—to climb the ladder of high society. "She had resolved to be an attractive and accomplished woman, even if she never became a great artist," Aunt Louisa tells us, after the three-year span that separates the two parts of *Little Women*. She describes Amy's flawed view of popularity in a way that translates perfectly into our culture, given our collective adulation of celebrity: "One of her weaknesses was a desire to move in 'our best society,' without being quite sure what the best really was. Money, position, fashionable accomplishments, and elegant manners were most desirable things in her eyes and she liked to associate with those who possessed them, often mistaking the false for the true, and admiring what was not admirable."

Amy endures several predicaments as a result of her desire to climb socially. After she invests time and hard-earned money to host an elegant lunch for a group of rich girls, only one of those invited attends, and Amy's efforts are wasted. Another danger is the inability to judge character. She caters to the aristocratic Mr. Tudor, the nephew of the third cousin to a living English lord, who "puts on airs, snubs his sisters, worries his father, and doesn't speak respectfully of his mother," as Jo tells her sister. As the girls argue over whether to be agreeable to men who have social status but lack character, Amy declares that a lack of status prevents the March girls from having an influence on people around them. Jo responds to her sister with sarcasm, saying, "That's a nice sort of morality." Still in vain pursuit of social status, an older Amy tries marrying into wealth and society. Tempted by the affections of Fred Vaughn, a debonair Brit who is "very rich and come[s] of an excellent family," she decides to accept his proposal even though she doesn't love him. She confesses this to Marmee in a letter, describing her desire for an "estate that's full of solid luxury . . . the family jewels, the old servants . . . park, great house, lovely grounds and fine houses."

Eventually, though, grief over Beth's decline, a longing for home, and a growing love for Laurie change her mind. After she turns down Fred's proposal, Aunt Louisa tells us that Amy "didn't care to be a queen of society now half so much as she did to be a lovable woman." Once Amy marries Laurie, her new husband teasingly questions her motives, since he, like Fred Vaughn, is wealthy and established. A mature Amy responds earnestly: "I forgot you were rich when I said 'Yes.' I'd have married you if you haven't had a penny, and I sometimes wish you *were* poor that I might show how much I love you."

In the novel's final chapter, we see that romantic love alone cannot fully bring about a lasting change in Amy's values. Only suffering accomplishes this. The frailty of their daughter is "a cross that Laurie and Amy bear together," and it is this pain that finally brings about a fundamental change in priorities. "Amy's nature was growing sweeter, deeper, and more tender; Laurie was growing more serious, strong, and firm; and both were learning that beauty, youth, good fortune, even love itself, cannot keep care and pain, loss and sorrow, from the most blest."

Jo's desire for worldly success is quite different from her sister's. She wants to do something splendid, heroic, or wonderful that won't be forgotten after her death. While she waits to discern what this contribution might be, she intends to "write books, and get rich and famous."

Jo starts off in pursuit of this ambition by writing the "class of light literature in which the passions have a holiday." Her father shakes his head when he reads her first published story and tries to convince her to steward her talent more wisely: "You can do better than this, Jo. Aim at the highest, and never mind the money." Next, Jo writes a novel that receives mixed reviews. Honest criticism begins to steer her vocation in the right direction, "for those whose opinion had real value gave her the criticism which is an author's best education; and when the first soreness was over, she could laugh at her poor little book, yet believe in it still, and feel herself the wiser and stronger for the buffeting she had received."

Despite this first lesson, Jo continues to publish seedy tales of passion, mostly for the money. Aunt Louisa doesn't condemn Jo—or herself, given the autobiographical nature of *Little Women*—for this motive. But she does show how pursuing fortune as a *first* motivation in vocation leads to compromise and a slow erosion of integrity and character: "She thought she was prospering finely; but unconsciously, she was . . . living in bad society; and, imaginary though it was its influence affected her, for she was feeding heart and fancy on dangerous and unsubstantial food."

Thankfully, something comes along to restrict this poor use of Jo's talent: she begins to care deeply about the opinion of Professor Bhaer, a man of integrity and intellect who describes sensational stories as "bad trash." Full of humiliation that he might discover her own "inflammable nonsense," Jo "stuff[s] the whole bundle into her stove, nearly setting the chimney afire with the blaze." After trying her hand at a "didactic gem" and a "child's story," she has a "fit of very wholesome humility," declaring, "I don't know anything; I'll wait till I do before I try again, and, meantime, 'sweep mud in the street,' if I can't do better; that's honest."

Temperance adds value to ambition. We see it bring satisfaction in Jo's vocation, as humbly writing in her true voice and dutifully providing for her family displace the earlier primacy she gave to fame and fortune. After a long period of mourning Beth, Jo begins to write again and pens a "story that [goes] straight to the hearts of those who read it." Her father submits it for her to a book publisher, and when it becomes a great success, he tells her, "You have found your style at last. You wrote with no thought of fame or money, and put your heart into it, my daughter; you have had the bitter, now comes the sweet." As with Amy, grief also plays a vital role in Jo's formation: "So, taught by love and sorrow, Jo wrote her little stories, and sent them away to make friends for themselves and her."

Moderating ambition doesn't mean we can't achieve great things during our relatively short time on the planet. Judging by the life of Aunt Louisa, Jo fulfilled her goal to do something wonderful that wouldn't be forgotten after her death. Here we are, more than a century after she died, still guided and formed by her writing.

At the close of the novel, Aunt Louisa's Marmee turns her experience of living a tempered, fruitful life into a blessing for readers in any age: "Touched to the heart, Mrs. March could only stretch out her arms, as if to gather children and grandchildren to herself, and say with face and voice full of motherly love, gratitude, and humility,—'O my girls, however long you may live, I never can wish you a greater happiness than this!'"

Perhaps that's why *Little Women* has endured as a classic: the hunger for a wholehearted life continues unabated. Despite the counterfeits offered by our self-indulgent, materialistic, success-obsessed culture, we long for the well-tempered life. Aunt Louisa's gift to us through the March family is the portrait of an alternative life that overflows with joy, peace, and love.

REFLECT AND DISCUSS

1. With which of the March sisters do you most identify? Why?
2. This chapter looks at how and why we should temper our desires for wealth, emotional expression, and ambition. What do harmful extremes in behavior and attitude look like when it comes to wealth, emotional expression, and ambition?

3. Aristotle taught that temperance means seeking a "golden mean" between extremes. In your socio-economic context and stage of life, how would you define the golden mean between your answers to question 2?

4. In which category—money, emotion, or career—are you farthest from that "golden mean"? And in which direction (too much focus or desire versus too little) do you tend toward?

5. Has any experience of suffering or loss affected the pursuit of these extremes in your life?

6. How might gratitude and generosity moderate your desire for luxury?

7. How might self-control and prayer moderate your emotions?

8. How might humility and filial duty moderate ambition in your career?

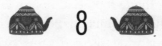

8

FAVORITISM AND JUSTICE

A LITTLE PRINCESS BY FRANCES HODGSON BURNETT

It just happened that I was born with a father who was beautiful and nice and clever, and could give me everything I liked. Perhaps I have not really a good temper at all, but if you have everything you want and everyone is kind to you, how can you help but be good-tempered?

—Sara Crewe

If someone forced me to decide which one of these seven novels influenced me most in childhood, I'd have to choose *A Little Princess* by Frances Hodgson Burnett (Aunt

Frances). This riches-to-rags-to-riches story of a winsome, imaginative British girl who leaves her soldier father behind in India to study at a boarding school in London (spoiler: and becomes another adoptee, although allowed to express some grief) captured my imagination from the start. I gained insight into the world's skewed values when befriending Sara Crewe for the first time, and my dislike of favoritism and desire for justice was reinforced with each subsequent reread.

Aunt Frances was also one of my first teachers in the practice of giving. One scene stands out in my memory. In the middle of the story, Sara has plummeted from wealth to poverty. She is trudging through a snowstorm, hungry and wet, when she finds a four-penny piece. Oh, how I rejoiced over that find! As she enters a baker's shop, though, Sara passes "a little figure more forlorn than herself . . . with big, hollow, hungry eyes." She buys four buns, and the kind baker adds two more. One by one, Sara places five buns in the other girl's lap, keeping only one for herself.

I remember being astounded by the gesture because at that point in the story, my heart was aching over Sara's suffering. And now my literary friend was giving away the food I had so wanted her to relish! But I knew it was the right thing to do. From then on, when I encountered hunger, I would remember that scene in *A Little Princess* and be stirred to respond. Eventually, I would choose to study political science and public policy with a focus on poverty as well as to explore themes of justice in my own writing for children.

As a parent, I read *A Little Princess* aloud to our twins when they were nine. When we reached the narrative about Sara giving away those fresh-baked pieces of bread, my voice quavered a bit, but I powered through to the end of the chapter. The room was quiet, filled with that listening stillness that every reading parent or teacher recognizes. Looking up, I saw the thoughtfulness in the boys' expressions and the compassion in their eyes. I didn't comment, and we moved on.

Once again, Aunt Frances's powerful story had accomplished its heart-shaping work.

COLONIALISM IN THE BONES OF A BOOK

As I read this book to our sons, however, I could see that it is one of the most problematic of my favorites to revisit in our era. Some educators and parents are recommending not reading it at all to children, mainly because of the way it portrays class, race, and colonial rule. Before we examine themes of favoritism and justice in this book, we need to take a closer look at these issues.

A REFORMER'S VIEW OF CLASS. *A Little Princess*, as we know it, was first published in 1905 during England's Edwardian era. But Aunt Frances wrote the bulk of it during the last years of the British Empire's Victorian era, after she had moved to the United States at age sixteen. A short story called "Sara Crewe, or What Happened at Miss Minchin's" was published as a series in a magazine in December 1887 and in book form in 1888. It's interesting to compare the original story, available for free online in the Gutenberg library, to the revised one that became *A Little Princess*, published in 1905. Aunt Frances introduced the character of Becky, a member of the exploited working class, and further humanized Ram Dass, the Indian servant who is instrumental in Sara's restoration. These changes, written after Aunt Frances's elder son Lionel died in 1900, deepened the complexity of the book and added nuance to the issues of class and race.

In Victorian and Edwardian England, "beggars" and "servants" served a rich, educated upper class without holding many rights themselves. But does Aunt Frances's novel promote this preferential treatment of the upper class? Not so much. The Labour Party was growing during the time that she wrote the story, and people in the working class were beginning to organize in unions. In 1905, when the revision was published, the author revealed the injustice of the system in a subversive way by adding the lovable, sympathetic character of Becky. When Sara, finding Becky asleep in her room, puts her hand against the servant girl's cheek, she has a deep realization that we as readers receive as well: "We are just the same—I am only a little girl like you. It's just an accident that I am not you, and you are not me."

Becky's capacity to love and care for Sara deeply before and after her reversal of fortune makes their friendship authentic and mutual, despite differences in class.

A NUANCED VIEW OF RACE. "Foreign" characters in white-centered stories sometimes show up as "exotic others" who save the day and then exit, without any backstory of their own. I recognized this common literary trope, even as a child, in the form of the mystical "lascar" servant, Ram Dass, who is instrumental in saving Sara from a life of abuse and poverty. Lascars were sailors from the Indian subcontinent and other Asian regions who worked on European ships. Atypically, though, in her revision, Aunt Frances allowed Ram Dass to reveal his name when he introduces himself to Sara as the helper in the house next door owned by a wealthy man named Mr. Carrisford. The author also gave us more time inside his head and heart: "The truth was the poor fellow felt as if his gods had intervened, and the kind little voice came from heaven itself." Later in the novel, adding a chapter fully devoted to Ram Dass, Aunt Frances describes him as "the intimate exponent of Sara, though she had only spoken to him once." We learn that he, like Sara, pays close attention to others before arriving at just conclusions (although he does sound like a personification of a deity in this passage):

> I see her when she does not see me. . . . I watch her from my window when she does not know I am near . . . the poor slave of the house comes to her for

comfort. There is a little child who comes to her in secret; there is one older who worships her and would listen to her forever if she might. . . . By the mistress of the house—who is an evil woman—she is treated like a pariah; but she has the bearing of a child who is of the blood of kings. . . . All her life each day I know. . . . Her going out I know, and her coming in; her sadness and her poor joys; her coldness and her hunger.

When he outlines his plan for blessing Sara, Ram Dass smiles "as if his heart warmed under his white robe." Aunt Frances's instinct as a writer was to make an Indian a real character, not a generic one, despite the fact that Carrisford's secretary jokingly casts him as a "magical Oriental" genie figure. I could easily imagine this foreigner as my own just and compassionate father, who endured intense loneliness and suspicion during his engineering studies in London. Baba's homesick heart would have danced if a British girl in a neighboring attic had spoken to him in Bangla; he would have wanted to make things right for her just as Ram Dass did.

The fact that Aunt Frances included a lascar in her story at all is striking. Indian sailors were exploited and marginalized in the London of her childhood, and they rarely show up as sympathetic characters in fiction written during that time. The vast majority worked as crew members on British merchant ships, recruited from maritime areas in the Indian subcontinent. By 1914, lascars made up more than 15 percent of the total number of mariners staffing British registered ships—about fifty-one thousand men. Typically, they were treated harshly and paid much less than European sailors. This leads us to a more compelling reason *A Little Princess* is problematic today: a flawed portrayal of colonialism.

BENEVOLENT COLONIALISM: AN OXYMORON. I'd love to make a case that Aunt Frances handled colonialism well simply because I love the book so much. But I can't. In my view, Aunt Frances's fiction reveals that she actually *didn't* favor colonialism—but only because of the negative consequences for British families who lived in India. She doesn't allocate space in her novels at all for the suffering of the Indians under British rule. Too bad, right?

Diamonds, the statue of Buddha, the furniture and brocades inherited by Sara from her Eton-trained father and "Uncle Tom" Carrisford: all these remind me of everything that was pillaged from India during British imperialism. The deferential title "sahib" used by Ram Dass and other Indians in Aunt Frances's writing makes my hackles rise, especially as I remember Baba's stories of fearing the "sha-heb," the word for white colonial rulers who were also sometimes called "ghosts" by my father and other villagers. I deeply dislike the salaaming and bowing by brown bodies that Sara, as the daughter of a British soldier in the Raj, took for granted.

I also reject the argument that colonialism brought benefits to India. From 1757 to India's independence in 1947—that is, during the entire period of British rule—there was no increase in per capita income within the Indian subcontinent. During the heyday of British rule, or the British Raj, from 1872 to 1921, Indian life expectancy dropped by 20 percent. Compare that with the seventy years or so since independence, during which Indian life expectancy increased by approximately twenty-seven years (66 percent). It's hard to argue that colonial rule was anything but devastating, even when you point to a few so-called gifts like India's education and railway systems. So how might a flawed book like *A Little Princess* shape the minds and hearts of children—especially Indian children—when it comes to viewing colonialism?

As I read the novel to our sons, I introduced them to British oppression in India and the independence movement led by Mahatma Gandhi and other resistance leaders. I recounted their grandparents' stories of surviving colonialism, war, and displacement. When the boys were nine, there wasn't much fiction for young readers written by authors of South Asian descent about colonialism and Partition. Today, they could have read historical novels published in the United States by Veera Hiranandani, Supriya Kelkar, Uma Krishnaswami, Kashmira Sheth, Padma Venkatraman,

FAVORITISM AND JUSTICE | 157

and others, including their mom. But such books weren't written yet. What I could do back then was begin to frame the questions about race, culture, and power we'll cover in chapter 10—questions I hope the adult versions of those little boys still ask about stories.

JUSTICE: THE OPPOSITE OF FAVORITISM

A Little Princess is an example of how an author may not see a lack of virtue—even one she cherishes—within her own social and historical context. Lodged as it is in a colonial mindset, some may think it ironic that Aunt Frances's novel provides such deep insight into justice. And yet it does. This virtue as defined by Thomas Aquinas is "a habit whereby man renders to each one his due by a constant and perpetual will." The *Catechism of the Catholic Church* elaborates on this definition:

> Justice is the moral virtue that consists in the con-
> stant and firm will to give their due to God and
> neighbor. . . . The just man, often mentioned in the
> Sacred Scriptures, is distinguished by habitual right
> thinking and the uprightness of his conduct toward
> his neighbor. "You shall not be partial to the poor or
> defer to the great, but in righteousness shall you judge
> your neighbor."

While the virtues of courage and temperance are focused on self, justice governs how we relate to others and to God. It stands opposed to partiality and favoritism.

Miss Minchin, the headmistress of the boarding school in London to which Sara is sent, is the poster child of favoritism. She treats people with more wealth, capacity, and status better than she treats those with less. She welcomes Captain Crewe by flattering his daughter because "she had heard that he was a rich father who was willing to spend a great deal of money on his little daughter." She fawns over wealthy Sara, giving her a sitting room and bedroom suite, a French maid, the most prestigious place in the school's seating arrangement, and a position at the head of the line during the school's Sunday walk to church. When Sara reminds Miss Minchin that Becky, the scullery maid, is also a little girl, Miss Minchin reveals her view of the "other"—in this case, people with lower status and power: "Scullery maids—er—are not little girls," she says. After Sara loses her wealth in a diamond mine fiasco, as well as the protection of her rich father, Miss Minchin treats her former show pupil as if she is nothing. "You are quite alone in the world, and have no one to do anything for you," she tells Sara coldly. "You are like Becky."

Our culture today is quintessentially Minchin-esque. Favoritism is rampant, and most of us would love to be on the receiving end of perks that only a few get. Nonprofits and academies host lavish banquets and getaways for high-end donors. Hotel elevators carry a chosen few to exclusive rooms on the penthouse level. Pharmaceutical companies fly doctors to tropical resorts for "conferences." Businesses send products to blue-checked social media stars in exchange for endorsements. Celebrities expect front-row seats and bags of swag when they attend events. First-class passengers board through their own red-carpeted entrances while the rest of us watch. Our culture has labels for people who receive special treatment, like "very important people" or VIPs, guests of honor, preferred, premium, executive, and platinum members.

Other incidences of favoritism are more insidious. A man's opinion is given more credence than a woman's. White Americans don't experience racial profiling in public, while Black men and women must stay guarded, especially during encounters with authorities. Spanish speakers who can't switch to English are overlooked and pushed aside. Foreign voices with non-European accents grate on some born-in-the-USA ears. The frail elderly, at-risk children, and people with different abilities are unseen and neglected. Meanwhile, people with status, connections, and wealth and those with strength, success, or a better education are treated preferentially.

In the Bible, Jesus's brother James made it clear that God forbids the practice of doling out favor to the powerful: "My brothers and sisters, believers in our glorious Lord Jesus Christ must not show favoritism. Suppose a man comes into your meeting wearing a gold ring and fine clothes, and a poor man in filthy old clothes also comes in. If you show special attention to the man wearing fine clothes and say, 'Here's a good seat for you,' but say to the poor man, 'You stand there' or 'Sit on the floor by my feet,' have you not discriminated among yourselves and become judges with evil thoughts?" (James 2:1–4).

But what about *receiving* favor? After all, it's not wrong to hanker for the special treatment a parent gives to a beloved child. I wish everybody could see what I saw each time I entered my father's presence: a face lighting up with joy at the sight of me. In *A Little Princess*, Sara Crewe also has a papa who gives her the unconditional favor that helps her resist the lure of Miss Minchin's false favoritism. Even if we didn't have human parents who gave us that gift, all of us share a divine parent who does. "The 'no matter whatness' of God dissolves the toxicity of shame and fills us with tender mercy," writes Father Gregory Boyle in his book *Tattoos on the Heart*. "Favorable, finally, and called by name—by the one your mom uses when she's not pissed off." Our culture offers conditional favor as a counterfeit version of God's unconditional love. People treat us with favor only when they want something in return, and we are tempted to do the same with others.

RESISTING FAVORITISM WITH THREE PRACTICES

Despite the pressure to participate in favoritism, in both the giving and the receiving of it, we can resist it. First, we notice when we are sought out and offered preferential treatment with conditions attached. Is someone—an organization or a person—courting our influence or wealth by pandering to our hankering for exclusive treatment? Are we being offered gifts, membership, or honor that isn't accessible to those with less power? The virtue of justice may call us to refuse such special favors altogether. If we do accept a gift or favor in exchange for an endorsement or donation, we might maintain our integrity by revealing the transaction openly, overcoming the temptation to keep it a secret. Even with the safeguard of transparency in place, however, one such transaction leads easily to another, and we may start down the slippery slope of addiction to special treatment.

The second way to resist favoritism is by paying attention on a daily basis to how we treat people who are devalued in our culture. In some challenging words about judgment, Jesus asked us to consider how we treat the "least of these" around us. You may want to read or reread Matthew 25:31–45 to see what he says. This requires taking stock of our interactions with a custodian at the office, the "accented" voice at a call center trying to help us with technology, the waiter at a restaurant, and the elderly person holding up the line at the grocery store. To expose this gross tendency, we notice where our gaze travels during encounters: are we making eye contact with the "least-seen" in our presence?

In Jesus's day, children were less-valuable members of society—as they are in our culture, judging by the low wages we pay to those who care for and teach them. But he affiliated himself with them as he did with people who are hungry, thirsty, in need of clothing, sick, incarcerated, and strangers: "Taking a child, He set him before them, and taking him in His arms, He said to them, 'Whoever receives one child like this in My name receives Me; and whoever receives Me does not receive Me, but Him who sent Me'" (Mark 9:36–37 NASB1995). Do we offer less honor and hospitality to a child than we would to a celebrity or politician?

A third practice that resists favoritism is to notice and confess jealousy when someone else is favored. A jealous response is personified in the character of Lavinia, who takes malicious pleasure in Sara's suffering. For me, jealousy rears its head in the world of publishing, where some authors receive prestigious awards, massive publicity, lucrative speaking gigs, and best-seller status while the rest of us plod on. When I see envy souring my spirit and comparison robbing me of joy, I know it is time to pray a dangerous prayer called A Litany of Humility. Here's a portion of it; pray it at your own risk.

O Jesus, meek and humble of heart,
Hear me.
From the desire of being esteemed,
Deliver me, O Jesus.
From the desire of being loved,
Deliver me, O Jesus.
From the desire of being extolled,
Deliver me, O Jesus.
From the desire of being honored,
Deliver me, O Jesus.
From the desire of being praised,
Deliver me, O Jesus.
From the desire of being preferred to others,
Deliver me, O Jesus.
From the desire of being consulted,
Deliver me, O Jesus.
From the desire of being approved,
Deliver me, O Jesus.
From the fear of being humiliated,
Deliver me, O Jesus.
From the fear of being despised,
Deliver me, O Jesus.
From the fear of suffering rebukes,
Deliver me, O Jesus.
From the fear of being calumniated,
Deliver me, O Jesus.

From the fear of being forgotten,
Deliver me, O Jesus.
From the fear of being ridiculed,
Deliver me, O Jesus.
From the fear of being wronged,
Deliver me, O Jesus.
From the fear of being suspected,
Deliver me, O Jesus.
That others may be loved more than I,
Jesus, grant me the grace to desire it.
That others may be esteemed more than I,
Jesus, grant me the grace to desire it.
That, in the opinion of the world, others may
increase and I may decrease,
Jesus, grant me the grace to desire it.
That others may be chosen and I set aside,
Jesus, grant me the grace to desire it.
That others may be praised and I go unnoticed,
Jesus, grant me the grace to desire it.
That others may be preferred to me in everything,
Jesus, grant me the grace to desire it.
That others may become holier than I, provided that
I may become as holy as I should,
Jesus, grant me the grace to desire it.

God tends to answer speedily, judging from my own experience. The results don't always feel good. But given that we are

immersed in a culture that promotes a vulgar way of assessing people, resisting our inner Minchin *and* our inner Lavinia on a daily basis is vital, and this prayer helps.

PRACTICING JUSTICE

We need to channel our inner Sara Crewe when it comes to taking stock of other people. Making judgments about others is something human beings do continually, and only justice enables us to do this well. Sara exemplifies the cardinal virtue of justice, exercising it when she recognizes flattery as deception. "She is beginning by telling a story," she observes, making her first evaluation of Miss Minchin. Her clear-eyed judgment continues throughout the novel, and she expresses her opinion of the school's owner after being told of her father's death:

> "Stop!" said Miss Minchin. "Don't you intend to thank me?"
>
> Sara paused, and all the deep, strange thoughts surged up in her breast.
>
> "What for?" she said.
>
> "For my kindness to you," replied Miss Minchin. "For my kindness in giving you a home."
>
> Sara made two or three steps toward her. Her thin little chest heaved up and down, and she spoke in a strange un-childishly fierce way.

"You are not kind," she said. "You are NOT kind, and it is NOT a home."

What a judgment! What truth! Sara has the ability to see intentions behind people's words and actions, a skill that comes from paying attention to others instead of focusing on how others see us. On her first day of school, she isn't "abashed at all by the many pairs of eyes watching her," but instead "she was interested and looked back quietly at the children who looked at her." Sara is wondering "what they were thinking of, and if they liked Miss Minchin, and if they cared for their lessons, and if any of them had a papa at all like her own." Might we, too, forget ourselves in a crowd by imagining the interior lives of others?

Sara's finely tuned sense of justice also causes her to feel angry on behalf of those who are unfairly treated: "It was a way of hers always to want to spring into any fray in which someone was made uncomfortable or unhappy." This habit of defending the underdog stems from noticing relationships between people. She watches Ermengarde carefully and ascertains her struggle to learn. When Lavinia, Jesse, and others laugh, "Sara tried to look as if she did not hear when Miss St. John called 'le bon pain,' 'lee bong pang.'" Why? Because justice and anger are comrades.

"Aquinas says that anger is the instrument of justice," writes Rebecca Konyndyk DeYoung in her book *Glittering Vices*. "Apathy is the tepid alternative to both love and anger." Sara is anything but apathetic: "She had a fine, hot little temper of her own, and it made her feel rather savage when she heard the titters and saw the poor, stupid, distressed child's face." When Lavinia accuses a frightened Becky of eavesdropping on Sara's storytelling, Sara feels "rather hot-tempered" and defends the scullery maid's right to listen. Justice requires us to practice the habit of standing up for the oppressed.

Sara also develops a just way of seeing as she grows in understanding of unmerited advantages, which we call "privileges" in today's discussions. Sara starts with many of them: she's clever, conversant in three languages, wealthy, healthy, and revered as the school's celebrity. She has been given her own handmaid, designer clothes, and a luxurious living space. Most of all, she has a parent who adores her and provides for her—one of the best privileges in the world. But Sara unpacks the power of those advantages with humility. Early in the story, she discerns a lack of connection between intellect and goodness: "Perhaps . . . to be able to learn things quickly isn't everything. To be kind is worth a great deal to other people. If Miss Minchin knew everything on earth and was like what she is now, she'd still be a detestable thing, and everybody would hate her. Lots of clever people have done harm and have been wicked."

She also comes to understand the refining power of adverse circumstances when it comes to character. "It just happened that I always liked lessons and books, and could remember things when I learned them," she tells Ermengarde. "It just happened that I was born with a father who was beautiful and nice and clever . . . I don't know . . . how I shall ever find out whether I am really a nice child or a horrid one. Perhaps I'm a *hideous* child, and no one will ever know, just because I never have any trials." After the privileges of wealth and comfort and status are gone, Sara sees that they did indeed mask a lack of love on her part. "You are nicer than I am," she confesses to Ermengarde, having assumed the worst of her friend. "I was too proud to try and make friends. You see, now that trials have come, they have shown that I am not a nice child. I was afraid they would."

Once Sara repents of her behavior to Ermengarde, she presses on through adversity to grow in justice. She offers hospitality, generosity, and courtesy to others regardless of their social status. Whether interacting with the grumpy cook, the small son in the wealthy Carmichael family, Ram Dass, Becky, or the starving child she encounters on the street, she remains gracious. "Everything can be taken from a man but one thing: the last of the human freedoms— to choose one's attitude in any given set of circumstances, to choose one's own way," wrote Viktor E. Frankl, who persisted in seeking moral victories even while imprisoned in a Nazi concentration camp. Always, and somewhat mysteriously, virtuous character traits are refined and revealed when one is under duress.

Throughout *A Little Princess*, Miss Minchin cannot provoke Sara to respond in anger or sorrow. In her writing, Aunt Frances shines a light on a truth about power: the inability to control a just person's morality enrages a tyrant. Sara is able to stay free by seeing and defining her own identity as a princess—the real key to the virtue of justice. When we see ourselves as children of royalty, we have no fear of despots even when under their dominion. We are true to the values of the kingdom even when we lose the advantages that once gave us power.

This was true of Jesus, who never swerved in his understanding of his identity as a child of God. Who can dole out justice in the Prince of Peace's kingdom? Only an omniscient ruler, someone who sees every hidden deed and secret intention. Jesus's perfect vision saw that no human heart was fully good. This led him to submit to death on the cross, a place where his privilege and God's favor were offered generously to every one of us. But in a historical era just as infected by favoritism as ours, Jesus's teaching and actions revealed his kingdom's strange reverse system of preference. This upside-down bias was evident in the words of his mother, Mary, who sang, "He has brought down the powerful from their thrones, and lifted up the lowly; he has filled the hungry with good things, and sent the rich away empty" (Luke 1:53 NRSV).

In his famous sermon on a mountain, Jesus preached that God delights in blessing the meek, poor, and brokenhearted. "The last shall be first, and the first last," he taught (Matthew

20:16 NASB1995). "It is easier for a camel to go through the eye of a needle, than for a rich man to enter the kingdom of God" (Matthew 19:24 NASB1995). His eyes sought out the ostracized woman with the flow of blood as his disciples were pushing him through a crowd to meet a powerful man's needs. They saw overlooked children who wanted to come near; a woman about to be stoned by those who thought they were perfectly just; and his friend Mary, who took a man's place to learn at her rabbi's feet.

A perfectly just king doesn't need the blindfold that Western culture places over impartial Lady Justice's eyes; his gaze lingers on those least preferred by the world. We who see ourselves as "little princes" and "little princesses" in his kingdom should do the same. Pope Francis discussed the concept of a "preferential option for the poor": "God's heart has a special place for the poor, so much so that he himself 'became poor' (2 Cor 8:9). He assured those burdened by sorrow and crushed by poverty that God has a special place for them in his heart: 'Blessed are you poor, yours is the kingdom of God' (Lk 6:20); he made himself one of them: 'I was hungry and you gave me food to eat,' and he taught them that mercy towards all of these is the key to heaven (cf. Mt 25:5ff.)."

Excellent judgment means moving toward the "least of these" and treating them with preference. Perhaps that's why Aunt Frances closes the novel by featuring the London waif

Sara encountered in the middle of the story. Her name, we learn, is Anne, and she has found a home. Now she is commissioned by Sara to become a giver herself. The scene ends with a moment of deep connection between two girls who see that we are all beggars in desperate need:

> The children stood and looked at each other for a few minutes; and then Sara took her hand out of her muff and held it out across the counter, and Anne took it, and they looked straight into each other's eyes.
>
> "I am so glad," Sara said. "And I have just thought of something. Perhaps Mrs. Brown will let you be the one to give the buns and bread to the children. Perhaps you would like to do it because you know what it is to be hungry, too."
>
> "Yes, miss," said the girl.
>
> And, somehow, Sara felt as if she understood her, though she said so little, and only stood still and looked and looked after her as she went out of the shop with the Indian gentleman, and they got into the carriage and drove away.

REFLECT AND DISCUSS

1. Did you have people who looked upon you with unconditional favor when you were a child?

Describe them. If you can't think of any, let the tears flow. Every child should experience the gaze of love.

2. If you were able to name a couple of people in your childhood who loved you like that, what were the loving nicknames they gave you?

3. Whether or not you're a person of faith, imagine God calling you by those names. How does hearing that from a divine voice make you feel?

4. Notice the instances in the book where Becky blesses and enriches Sara's life. Take stock of your relationships. Do you have a friendship with a "Becky" in your life? Alternatively, perhaps you are a Becky to somebody else's Sara. What qualities in a relationship across boundaries of power lead to mutuality of exchange?

5. Read again the passage about Sara's interaction with the hungry child. Are there differences between giving and sacrificial giving? Have you attempted the latter?

6. Starting with the privileges enjoyed by Sara before her father died, list some unmerited favors you were given in childhood. Did you lose a few you once had as you've grown older? Or gained any that are new?

7. Have you transacted with a person or an organization courting your wealth or influence with

favoritism? If so, do other people know about the honor or gift you received?

8. Pay attention to recent encounters with people who could be called "the least of these." How have you treated people with less power? Upon whom have your eyes focused in public settings?

9. Confess to another person or to your group any jealousy you have been feeling. If you're feeling brave, pray the Litany of Humility alone or together. Be ready to note and share how God answers.

9

RASHNESS AND PRUDENCE

The Silver Chair by C. S. Lewis

And the signs which you have learned here will not look at all as you expect them to look, when you meet them there. That is why it is so important to know them by heart and pay no attention to appearances. Remember the signs and believe the signs. Nothing else matters.

—Aslan

When I read the Narnia series as a child, I saw myself as Lucy, thrilling to Aslan's voice because something about it reminded her of her own father's voice. I, too, was seeing my loving Baba in the great lion who ruled Narnia benevolently. I read all seven books again and again, enjoying the humor and wonder woven into each adventure. By the age of ten, I wanted to become friends with the author. I imagined taking a trip into a Narnian forest to spot elusive unicorns, with "Mr. Lewis" as my chosen companion. In the scene written in my diary, the two of us engaged in convivial chat as colleagues on the hunt for wonderful creatures like Jewel in *The Last Battle*. We even shared a pair of binoculars. The author of my favorite fantasy series was a trusted fictional uncle, and looking back, it's easy to see that he taught me much about goodness. The confidence I placed in him and in the Narnia books as a child is why I was so troubled by the racial and cultural issues I began to see as a young adult.

A CHALLENGING CONVERSATION WITH UNCLE JACK

Author Philip Pullman has described the Narnia series as one of the most blatantly bigoted books ever written. The "other" is indeed carved deeply into the structure of the Narnia series in the form of the Calormene people. We first meet this group of people in *The Voyage of the Dawn Treader*, the third book published in the Narnia series: "The Calormenes have dark faces and long beards. They wear flowing robes and orange-coloured turbans, and they are a wise, wealthy, courteous, cruel and ancient people." Later we learn they wear wooden shoes with an upturned toe and wield scimitars as weapons. They value honor, elders, power, and their ancient poets. Apart from worshipping a more Hindu-like deity of Tash, Calormen sounds much like the Turkish Ottoman Empire that rose to power in 1299, ruled for six centuries, and was defeated and dismantled by the allies at the end of World War I.

While I didn't identify as one of these turbaned foreigners, the color of my skin means I'd be more likely to be mistaken for a Calormene than any kin to "golden-haired" Lucy. Nowadays, in my imaginary conversations with the author of my beloved Narnia books, I ask difficult questions.

"Professor Lewis—"

"Call me Uncle Jack."

"Okay, then. Uncle Jack, why did you create a villainous, dark-skinned race at war with the noble, fair-skinned Narnians?"

I imagine him taking a deep breath. "My dear Mitali, you must remember that I was born in 1898 and grew up in the British Raj. I also fought in a war, which was devastating. The Ottoman Empire was a brutal enemy."

"I know that was a difficult time for you," I say, trying to sound sympathetic. But I don't let him out of the hot seat. "Did you have to say they were *all* cruel?"

"In my defense, I did feature a few excellent Calormene characters such as Emeth at the end of *The Last Battle*. They're only briefly mentioned in *The Voyage of the Dawn Treader*—in one scene as slave buyers—and they make no appearance at all in *The Magician's Nephew* or *The Silver Chair*, apart from a passing reference to the possibility of Narnia preparing for war in the latter. And please notice that in *A Horse and His Boy*, Aravis is a strong brown girl who escapes child marriage and marries interracially."

"Yes, but to achieve power and freedom, she must lose her home and family and become part of 'English' culture," I respond. "How am I supposed to read that to a class full of brown children?"

I can see Uncle Jack getting into professorial mode. "Perhaps educators may teach the books by describing Calormen as a symbol for large, powerful autocratic nations and Narnia as a stand-in for smaller countries in danger of being oppressed." He might even elaborate on this defense, echoing arguments presented by renowned Lewis scholars.

I'm not ready for excuses. "We could—if you hadn't described their skin color as dark and Narnians as fair-skinned. This makes it too much like our own world from British colonial eyes. Didn't you picture a girl like me reading your books when you wrote them?"

At that point in our imaginary conversation, I think he'd stop trying to prove that the books are ism-free. After writing them, he had married Joy Davidman, a Jewish woman who had once been a communist and was a thoughtful intellectual.

I wonder if she challenged him in the same way I'd like to. If she had, he might respond with this: "Joy did tell me that I should have handled that thread in the stories more deftly. I can see that now."

"If you could, Uncle Jack, would you go back in time to change them?"

"I wish I could go back and change much more than that mistake," he says, shaking his head. "We have a strange illusion that mere time cancels sin. I have heard others, and I have heard myself, recounting cruelties and falsehoods committed in boyhood as if they were no concern of the present speaker's, and even with laughter. But mere time does nothing either to the fact or to the guilt of a sin. The guilt is washed out not by time but by repentance and the blood of Christ: if we have repented these early sins we should remember the price of our forgiveness and be humble."

That last bit of dialogue is lifted directly from his writing, and it does help me forgive him. I imagine that, like the other writers we have come to know in this book, Uncle Jack might look back at his work and wince and squirm over errors—at least once someone (especially his beloved wife) pointed them out. The pain of mistakes made in the past is a good way to acquire prudence, a virtue venerated by the creator of the Narnia books.

THE CHARIOTEER QUEEN

When he discussed all seven virtues in the BBC radio shows that eventually became his book *Mere Christianity*, Uncle Jack said, "Prudence means practical common sense, taking the trouble to think out what you are doing and what is likely to come of it." I learn about prudence each time I read *The Silver Chair* in the Narnia series. This fourth book in the Chronicles of Narnia features two English children, Jill Pole and Eustace Scrubb, who are sent on a quest by Aslan, the great lion, to find a lost prince of Narnia. Along the way, the children make a series of rash decisions. Meanwhile, their Narnian guide, Puddleglum the Marshwiggle, an anthropomorphic creature who dwells in the marshes and has frog-like qualities, serves as a personification of prudence.

The word *prudence* is no longer used much in our culture. Baby boomers hear the word and think of an outdated British woman's name, referring to someone John Lennon invited out to play in the Beatles' song "Dear Prudence." Some of my peers also remember a *Saturday Night Live* skit in which the comedian Dana Carvey made fun of President George W. Bush for saying, "It wouldn't be prudent at this juncture." But apart from a few pop culture connections, we rarely hear or speak the word.

Younger adults sometimes react negatively to it, as they think it is connected to *prude*: "A person who is excessively or priggishly attentive to propriety or decorum . . . especially a woman who shows or affects extreme modesty," according to *Merriam-Webster*. But the two words are unrelated etymologically. *Prude* comes from the French *prudefemme* (good woman), but *prudent* comes from the Latin *prudens*, a contraction of *pro* (forward) and *videre* (to see). So *prudence* literally means "to see ahead." Although out of vogue, prudence is well worth reencountering today, by both the young and the old, because it helps us decide how to act in the moment and to consider future consequences.

Prudence, according to the ancients, is the *auriga virtutum*, or charioteer, of the virtues. The task of prudence is to decide which of the others should be put to use in determining a course of action in a particular circumstance. Prudence warns courage to consider what justice might require, invites justice to weigh in on what love might say, asks temperance to wonder if justice demands bold speech instead of restraining the tongue, and so on. It is the commanding voice of a woman driving a chariot—one who says "Woah!" or "Giddyap!" to the six horses of virtue and encourages them to move forward together.

Prudence slows us down when we're tempted to move too quickly. Oh, how we need her caution in a time of impulsive, thoughtless action and reaction that results in damaged lives. Companies, politicians, leaders, and everyday social media influencers are expected to speak out quickly in response to an accusation or a problem and to do so without hesitation. Individuals get riled up in response to current or personal events and rashly hit "send" or "post"—*before* giving prudence a chance to moderate and guide.

But is prudence always conservative, recommending restraint before we take action? No. Sometimes the virtue speeds us up, moving us to passionate deeds, like overturning tables and clearing out commerce as Jesus did when he discovered profiteering in the temple. Prudence has helped great leaders throughout history bring about social change, harnessing courage to act or speak boldly, providing justice to see people and situations without favoritism, recommending temperance when emotions grew heated, and calling in faith, hope, and love in the midst of defeat, alienation, persecution, and incarceration.

Whether prudence slows us down or calls us to rise up and act, the queen of virtues steers us to choose the right actions at the right time with the right motivations. As with the other virtues, we practice prudence in smaller decisions so when we need it for the big ones, it will be strong enough to rise up and coordinate the other virtues. Ignatius of Loyola's *Spiritual Exercises* provides a way to build prudence. He encourages us to practice the examen: a period of reflection typically in the evening, during which we pay attention to our emotional lives by recognizing times of desolation and consolation we've experienced throughout the day. We also reflect on decisions made, both good and bad, confessing errors in judgment and failure to love. The result, hopefully, is prudence.

When Jill and Eustace first start journeying with Puddleglum, they see him as a "wet blanket," dampening enthusiasm, pointing out pitfalls, and overstating the possible negatives. This is how the voice of prudence is first heard in our cultural context: as somewhat bossy and dour. We may resist it at first, but soon we begin to hear that voice differently. The character of Puddleglum reveals how this virtue guides us when we are embroiled in useless dissension, led astray by distraction, or nearly devastated by deception.

USELESS DISSENSION

One of the things I like about the Narnia books is how Uncle Jack candidly describes quarreling. *The Silver Chair* is no exception. "Shut up!" Jill tells Eustace. "Dry up," Eustace retorts. "Don't keep interrupting." She calls him a perfect beast and an ass. He calls her a fool and accuses her of nearly murdering him. Ah, so human. This sort of argument and blame is what we find on social media and in offices, churches, political entities, and homes. Quarreling makes us forget our shared quests as a family, organization, nation, or planet—which include to heal, nourish, restore, illuminate, season, bless, repair, defend, forgive, and create.

When the children fight, prudence in the form of Puddle-glum warns of what might happen: "Won't do to quarrel, you know. At any rate, don't begin it too soon. I know these expeditions usually end that way: knifing one another, I shouldn't wonder, before all's done. But the longer we can keep of it—"

This is a cynical but wise prediction, connecting fighting and insults to murder as Jesus did in the Sermon on the Mount (see Matthew 5:21–24). The children can easily remember the last time they fought at the edge of the cliff, when Jill almost did kill Eustace. Later, Puddleglum stops the children from arguing over a sword and knife by saying, "Ah, there you are. I thought as much. That's what usually happens on adventures." This shuts both of them up. Like the Marshwiggle, the virtue of prudence draws on temperance to keep us from escalating an argument to the next rash response.

TIME-WASTING DISTRACTION

Prudence also tries to rescue us when the narrow uphill path of trying to be and do good becomes arduous and a wider, easier road distracts us. In the midst of any movement away from God, this virtue invites faith to help us obey God's commands. Puddleglum does the same, reminding Jill of Aslan's instructions. Just as God gave the greatest commandment along with the rest of the law to the people of Israel and told them to remember these through repetition (see Deuteronomy 6:4–9), Aslan gave Jill four signs to help the children achieve their quest, along with strict instructions to memorize them:

> Remember, remember, remember the signs. Say them to yourself when you wake in the morning and when you lie down at night, and when you wake in the middle of the night. . . . Here on the mountain I have spoken to you clearly; I will not often do so down in Narnia. . . . And the signs which you have learned here will not look at all as you expect them to look, when you meet them there. That is why it is so important to know them by heart and pay no attention to appearances. Remember the signs and believe the signs. Nothing else matters.

When the children and Puddleglum meet the Lady of the Green Kirtle and her silent, armored companion on the bridge, Jill rashly shares Aslan's first sign, telling these newcomers that they are on the hunt for the ruined city of the giants. Puddleglum stops her before she can share the rest of them and tries to change the subject: "We'd as soon not talk to strangers about our business, if you don't mind. Shall we have a little rain soon, do you think?" The heedless trust of an attractive someone who *appears* to have our best interests in mind is countered by prudence, reminding us to exercise justice over favoritism.

Typically, the temptation to pursue a different destination than the virtuous life intensifies along the way. When weary, cold travelers hear about hot baths, comfortable beds, and roaring fires, and hungry children imagine roast beef and cakes served up four times a day, it's hard to resist, especially on an arduous journey shaped by suffering and self-sacrifice. Jill and Eustace are distracted by the sweet-voiced and beautiful Lady of the Green Kirtle's suggestion to visit the Gentle Giants of Harfang. Puddleglum, however, continues to personify prudence by protesting the visit to Harfang, arguing that Aslan's signs hadn't mentioned anything about staying with giants. The cold, wet, and travel-weary children remain fixated on visiting the so-called Gentle Giants.

In stressful times, when internal (or external) voices tempt us to doubt God's guidance or indulge our needs and desires, prudence tries to remind us that faith and temperance lead to the good life. But as missed luxuries and pleasures gleam brightly in our imaginations, prudence resembles a fun-killing Marshwiggle. The children now can think of nothing but cozy beds, hot food, and warm fires. They stop talking about Aslan and their quest to find the lost prince. And Jill stops repeating the signs to herself every night and morning, a habit she's maintained throughout the journey until now.

It's easy to forget the "signs" when the virtuous life becomes difficult. We're tempted to pursue ease instead of obedience, but prudence keeps trying to help us stay the course:

> It was absolute misery to come back into the withering coldness. And it did seem hard when Puddleglum chose that moment for saying: "Are you still sure of those signs, Pole? What's the one we ought to be after now?"
>
> "Oh come on! Bother the signs," said Pole. "Something about someone mentioning Aslan's name, I think. But I'm jolly well not going to give a recitation here."

Jill, irritated at herself that she can't recount Aslan's instructions as well as she used to, gets the order wrong. Puddleglum continues talking, but the children don't listen. Jill even interrupts him and tells *him* to shut up—something she's said previously to Eustace but never to the Marshwiggle. Her command doesn't work. Just as Puddleglum doesn't stop trying, so prudence refuses to abandon us.

A refusal to listen to Puddleglum eventually leads the children to two horrifying consequences: they are imprisoned and about to be eaten by the giants of Harfang, and they have disobeyed and forgotten Aslan's instructions. Once they see the truth, repent, and escape, they find themselves deep in the disheartening darkness of Underworld, where they meet again the man who had been with the Lady of the Green Kirtle. Thankfully, Puddleglum is still with them, serving as guide and companion: "The children huddled close together on each side of Puddleglum. They had thought him a wet blanket while they were still above ground, but down here he seemed the only comforting thing they had."

Puddleglum suggests staying with the man while he is bound to a silver chair in a daily time of deep enchantment. The Marshwiggle is the one also to remind the children that the stranger's use of the name of Aslan in begging for freedom is the fourth sign. Acknowledging that the consequences might be dire, Puddleglum points out that Aslan asked only for obedience without guaranteeing positive outcomes. This time, the children listen to their guide. They cut the cords that bind the captive to the chair, and the man reveals his true identity to them as the son of King Caspian. Their quest is almost fulfilled, thanks to the prudence of Puddleglum. Evil, however, doesn't give up easily. When dissension and distraction don't succeed in hindering us, deception is the next move.

DEVASTATING DECEPTION

Uncle Jack wove Plato's allegory of the cave into several of his Narnia books, as do many other writers of books and screenplays. This philosophy of the nature of belief is a metaphor for the imprisonment of relying only on knowledge to see the world. In the allegory, prisoners are chained together in a cave. Behind them is a fire they can't see, and between the fire and the prisoners are people carrying puppets or other objects. These figures cast shadows on the side of the cave's wall, which is the only thing visible to the prisoners. They watch the shadows and believe that they are real. But one prisoner breaks loose, sees the fire, realizes the shadows are fake, escapes, and discovers a whole world outside the cave. Tragically, he is blinded because his eyes aren't used to sunlight. When he returns to try to free the other prisoners, they see his injury and refuse to leave the cave for fear of being blinded themselves.

In *The Lion, the Witch, and the Wardrobe*, when Peter and Susan doubt Lucy's veracity about the existence of an unseen world, Professor Diggory Kirke responds with a logical argument about her truthfulness and encourages them to give their younger sister the benefit of the doubt. "It's all in Plato, all in Plato: bless me, what do they teach them at these schools!" he says. In *The Last Battle*, dwarves thrown into the Stable that is so much more than a stable sit in a tight circle, refusing to see it as anything but a small, smelly place for animals. Even Aslan, with the gifts he tried to give, could not convince them otherwise:

Aslan raised his head and shook his mane. Instantly a glorious feast appeared on the Dwarfs' knees:

pies and tongues and pigeons and trifles and ices, and each Dwarf had a goblet of good wine in his right hand. But it wasn't much use. They began eating and drinking greedily enough, but it was clear that they couldn't taste it properly. They thought they were eating and drinking only the sort of things you might find in a Stable. One said he was trying to eat hay and another said he had got a bit of an old turnip and a third said he'd found a raw cabbage leaf. And they raised golden goblets of rich red wine to their lips and said, "Ugh! Fancy drinking dirty water out of a trough that a donkey's been at! Never thought we'd come to this."

But very soon every Dwarf began suspecting that every other Dwarf had found something nicer than he had, and they started grabbing and snatching, and went on to quarreling, till in a few minutes there was a free fight and all the good food was smeared on their faces and clothes or trodden under foot. But when at last they sat down to nurse their black eyes and their bleeding noses, they all said: "Well, at any rate, there's no Humbug here. We haven't let anyone take us in. The Dwarfs are for the Dwarfs!"

"You see," said Aslan. "They will not let us help them. They have chosen cunning instead of belief. Their prison is only in their own minds, yet they are in that prison; and so afraid of being taken in that they can not be taken out."

Plato's cave allegory and the prison of a "knowledge-only" view of reality also make an appearance in *The Silver Chair*. While the Witch wields magic powder, fire, and lies to convince the four humans that the Overworld of Narnia is a dream, Puddleglum keeps fighting for self-control. He uses temperance to resist the magic, remembering his own experience in Narnia and insisting stoutly that he had been there once. His words arouse his companions, but the Witch keeps asking questions with soft, silvery laughter, telling them there is "no Narnia, no Overworld, no sky, no sun, no Aslan." Soon, the Prince and the two children, in a trancelike state, lose their strength. They are almost wholly deceived.

Now Puddleglum calls upon the virtue of courage to stamp on the fire with his bare foot. This bold act of sacrifice changes everything: instead of the sweet, cooing voice of enchantment and the soothing fragrance of the powder, the room is full of the smell of burnt flesh and the loud, terrible voice of the enraged Witch. Puddleglum, his mind cleared by the shock of pain, marshals the virtue of faith: "I'm on Aslan's side even if there isn't any Aslan to lead it. I'm going to live as like a Narnian as I can even if there isn't any Narnia," he says. His deed and declaration break the spell on the others. It is his sword, along with the Prince's, that fells the evil serpent. In the same way, prudence valiantly fights for us, harnessing courage, faith, and the other virtues to defeat deception about what is real and true.

"You've been the best friend in the world," Eustace tells their companion at the end of *The Silver Chair*. Likewise, when our own quests for a fruitful life come to an end, we will acknowledge how prudence called upon the other virtues to help us, even through dissension, distraction, and deception. But we have to remember the signs. "Love the Lord your God with all your heart and with all your soul and with all your mind," our version of Aslan told us in Matthew 22.

REFLECT AND DISCUSS

1. Have you been quarreling with someone, even in your head? What are a couple of virtues prudence might involve to help you act or speak in the midst of dissension?

2. Do you ever grow weary at times in pursuit of a virtuous life? What other destinations sometimes seem more attractive, and why?

3. Are you distracted from the arduous journey of obedience by the promise of false comforts? If so, what

are they? Which commandments help your feet stay on the right path?

4. How is our culture like Plato's cave?
5. What are a few common deceptions that keep people around us captive in darkness and despair?
6. How might we emulate Puddleglum to resist these deceptions and help others see? Which of the other virtues are needed in this effort?

10

SEE THE FLAWS, SEEK THE VIRTUES

CONSUMING AND CREATING CHILDREN'S STORIES

If we want to lead children to think critically about stories, including seeing biases about race, culture, and power, we have to develop that kind of discernment ourselves. It takes work, but opportunities to grow in this skill abound. We can practice it with any book we consume, whether contemporary or ancient. All stories are didactic by nature because people with particular beliefs or unbelief create them. Newbery Medal–winning children's book author Katherine Paterson describes how faith shapes our work, whether or not we are aware of it:

I think it was [C. S.] Lewis who said something like: "The book cannot be what the writer is not." What you are will shape your book whether you want it to or not. I am Christian, so that conviction will pervade the book even when I make no conscious effort to teach or preach. Grace and hope will inform everything I write. . . . Self-consciously Christian (or Jewish or Muslim) writing will be sectarian and tend to propaganda and therefore have very little to say to persons outside that particular faith community. The challenge for those of us who care about our faith and about a hurting world is to tell stories which will carry the words of grace and hope in their bones and sinews and not wear them like fancy dress.

In creating the "bones and sinews" of a story, beliefs and biases in the mind of the creators play a major role. As Paterson points out, the subconscious depths are even more powerful than the conscious mind.

When it comes to stories for young people, I hone my critical thinking by asking questions about race, culture, and power. Below are eight of the most common; they are not a complete list in a discernment process, but they get me started. I hope they help you and the young people you love begin to see blatant as well as subliminal messages in the "bones and sinews" of stories, both classic and contemporary.

1. HOW IS RACE DEFINED, IF AT ALL?

An author might choose not to label or define race or culture with specific descriptors or phrases such as *Black* or *Indian American*. One reason these terms don't show up is if the book is set in a particular context where people of only one race or ethnicity dwell. My novels *Tiger Boy* and *Rickshaw Girl*, for example, are set in the villages of Bengal and contain only Bengali characters, so I felt no need to clarify with descriptors.

Another reason to omit racial definitions or labels is to create space for the imagination, giving readers the power to cast the characters. Have you ever been disappointed by a cinematic adaptation of a book because an actor playing a character on screen looked different than how that character appeared in your mind's eye? What could go wrong if authors omit racial descriptors so that readers can "see" characters any way they choose? One answer is that any ethnicity apart from whiteness might be erased. Without the author providing outright cues, most readers in a majority-white setting might default to seeing an all-white ensemble.

Even when the story does include specifics about race, however, countering readers' white default isn't solely in a writer's hands. Suzanne Collins, for example, clearly described Rue's satiny dark skin in the *Hunger Games* trilogy, making her character's race explicit. Some white-defaulting fans chose not to see those details in their reading and protested the casting of Black actors in the adaptation.

Defining race is trickier when a book uses a third-person instead of a first-person narrator. We might encounter a few race terms, as in *Harry Potter and the Sorcerer's Stone* by J. K. Rowling, when the narrator introduces Dean Thomas and other characters as "black." But when this omniscient voice labels only one person by race, we end up again with a white default for the characters who don't get a race attribution. Also, as the culture and language change, socially constructed race terms may become outdated or sound violent and hateful to the ear.

Maybe a character self-identifies racially (usually in dialogue), is identified by the first-person narrator of the story, or is described by another character (also usually in dialogue). If any of these happen, an astute reader asks a follow-up question or two. If a flawed character or narrator talks about race pejoratively, does the author make it clear that such bias is wrong? Or is such bias in—say it with me—the *bones* of the story (by now I'm sure you're thinking of Katherine Paterson's brilliance when you hear that refrain in this book). Is it emanating from conscious or unconscious biases from the author's social and historical context, as we talked about with *Anne of Green Gables*, *A Little Princess*, and the Narnia series?

Proper names and cultural details can also reveal race and ethnicity, but a diligent author will take the time to learn particulars. The Patil twins in *Harry Potter*, for example, are never labeled as originating in Maharashtra, Karnataka, Andhra Pradesh, or Telangana—places where that surname is commonly spelled with an *i* instead of an *e*. I wondered why the name wasn't anglicized as the more typical "Patel," a spelling used by Gujaratis who emigrated widely throughout the West. As Gujaratis, the sisters would drape the loose end of their Yule Ball sarees from back to front, as is common in that part of India, instead of front to back as in other parts of India. Cultural words about food, decor, or fashion may help define race and ethnicity, but storytellers must go beyond the generic to understand and convey specifics.

Another trick to notice is the use of accent or diction. The problem is when the sound of someone's English is a lazy shortcut to characterize, as many casting agencies seem to do in the realm of film and video games. The sophisticated and powerful evil genius character with an upper-class British accent is still prevalent in North American entertainment. Russian or Chinese accents are often used to signify villainous intent, and Indian accents are thrown in for humor or to offer medical advice. We see it in books as well. Flipping through a pile of review copies on my desk, I find one protagonist bothered by an antagonist's "metallic Southern drawl that grates on her consciousness." Cue our country's false, often negative view of regional accents from southern states. Japanese writers of manga rely on regional differences in language to send messages to their readers, using the Osaka dialect to signal that a character is funny and earthy. Accent or diction may emphasize that a character is newer to America, or older, or more traditional, but is the author relying on positive or negative stereotypes they assume we share about those groups to get us to root for or against a character?

It's vital for authors to explore the race and culture of characters *before* sharing stories with readers so that those realities sink into the structure of a story during the writing process. Hopefully, through this behind-the-scenes work, a writer can make the race and culture of characters overtly—and covertly—clear. But writers are only half of the conversational equation; stories by nature belong also to readers, who also bring deep-seated beliefs and prejudices. While reading a novel, we can assess the author's techniques in defining race and ethnicity. Are they creative and thoughtful? Or do they seem inadvertent and clunky?

When reading books with my students, I invite them to imagine two or three different racial or cultural identities for the characters. Does changing those change the story? Is it even possible to make such a change given the author's definitions or descriptors? How do we feel about switching around the characters' identities? Discussing these kinds of questions builds a habit of paying attention to overt or subliminal bias in stories, authors, and ourselves.

2. DOES THE STORY INCLUDE A TROPE INSTEAD OF A CHARACTER?

The word *trope* has come to describe commonly recurring literary and rhetorical devices, motifs, or clichés in stories. Racial tropes come out of our troubled history and are easy to see in stories from the past. Remember the Black actors who voiced the vagrant crows in Disney's *Dumbo*? And the chimpanzees who "want to be like you" in *The Jungle Book*? As discussed previously with accents, lazy storytellers use tropes as a shortcut to inform readers how to feel about characters. Blatantly racist, we think today, and feel morally indignant.

Nowadays, though, we see a hypercorrection that's just as lazy: a trend in signifying "evil" with a white character and "good" with a nonwhite character. Oh, quit whining, you might be thinking; at least we're finally seeing heroes who aren't of European descent! That's true. But I object to using *any* aspect of a character's ethnic or racial identity to signal virtue *or* vice. Tropes don't require us to know characters deeply.

In North American stories, a trope is sometimes a "Magical Negro" who aids or fleshes out the protagonist's character. Director and screenwriter Spike Lee lambasted this technique twenty years ago, according to Susan Gonzalez: "A 'new phenomenon' has emerged in film in recent years, in which an African-American character is imbued with special powers . . . but this new image is just a reincarnation of the same old stereotype or caricature of African Americans as the 'noble savage' or the 'happy slave' that has been presented in film and on television for decades, contended Lee. The film director . . . (asked) his audience the question: 'How is it that black people have these powers but they use them for the benefit of white people?'" At times, this trope is a loving mammy figure, hearkening to the Black nannies who taught white children to say "you is smart, you is kind, you is important." In other stories, "Mystical Orientals" are thrown in to guide the way, like Ram Dass in *A Little Princess*.

Tropes don't have a past or a future; they appear and disappear according to the main character's need. Does it seem as if an author has given thought to the secondary characters' history and motivations? Even if there isn't space in the story to include those details, ask which characters seem *real*. The rest, then, are tropes inserted into the story to serve the "real" characters, perhaps reinforcing a message of marginalization to readers who share that character's racial or cultural identity.

3. HOW IS BEAUTY DEFINED?

Throughout the world, "whiteness" has been venerated when it comes to standards of beauty because people of color lacked power, especially during colonialism. Dr. Huberta Jackson-Lowman writes about how this continues to shape a marginalized child's view of herself: "Perhaps the most insidious effect of white supremacy racism has been its impact on how people of color view their physical appearance . . . the globalization of Eurocentric standards of beauty has resulted in the development of industries that support it, the marketing of images that reify it, the structuring of policies that reward it, and the enactment of interpersonal and personal behavioral routines that emulate it."

A pursuit of "whiteness" in appearance is still common throughout the world. For example, a popular "fold surgery" creates an area in the eyelid for Asian girls to apply eye shadow. This is an effort to make them look more Caucasian, which supposedly provides an advantage in society. Lighter skin is prized in countries throughout Asia, Latin America, and Africa, where skin-bleaching creams are best-selling beauty products. When I watch Bengali-language television with my mother, we see ads touting the ability of such products to secure a mate or job. Thanks to a growing global awareness of the damage done by colorism, or shadism, this may be changing. The makers of Fair & Lovely skin cream in India changed the product's name to Glow & Lovely in response to protests. I've yet to see a dark-skinned person used in the advertisements, but hopefully that, too, will come.

False ideas of what makes a person attractive pepper a culture's stories. We can notice them with our children to lessen the damage they cause. Hone in on descriptions of physical beauty in a book. Do the pictures or words portray an attractive character with attributes associated only with people of European descent? Long, silky hair and large, wide eyes, for example, imply "not Black" and "not Asian." We can bring such messages about beauty into the light to be evaluated and resisted.

4. WHO IS THE INTENDED AUDIENCE?

A clue about a publisher's intended audience is when the cover art doesn't match the descriptions inside the book. Consider best-selling author Ursula K. Le Guin's perspective: "The characters are white. Even when they aren't white in the text, they are white on the cover. I know, you don't have to tell me about sales! I have fought many cover departments on this issue, and mostly lost. But please consider that 'what sells' or 'doesn't sell' can be a self-fulfilling prophecy. If Black kids, Hispanics, Indians both Eastern and Western, don't buy fantasy—which they mostly don't—could it be because they never see themselves on the cover?" Le Guin won the battle over her novel *Powers* when the publisher changed the final cover art from what the advance review copy featured on the cover to a cover that reflected the protagonist's Himalayan ancestry.

Another sign that the targeted buyer is white is when the main character is depicted as *more* foreign than the author describes in the text. Nowhere in Cynthia Kadohata's novel *Weedflower*, for example, does the protagonist wear a kimono. On the cover, however, she does. Why did the powers-that-be choose to make Sumiko look more Japanese than American? To sell more books during Asian Pacific American Heritage Month? To lure readers on the hunt for books about the "exotic other?" To me, a girl in jeans and a T-shirt behind barbed wire would have made the book more historically accurate and more interesting, but I don't work in marketing.

Titles also offer a clue to the intended audience. I've seen contemporary books for young people called *Illegal* or *Unwanted*. Apparently, undocumented or refugee children themselves aren't supposed to consume those stories. How would they respond to a book that labels them with such pejorative adjectives?

With every book for young readers, I notice cover art and word choices in the titles and jacket copy. Is it written for consumption by the powerful? I might still choose to read or give that book to a child, but I always want to model discernment—a practice that nudges the shared power of a story from creators to consumers.

5. IS THE PROTAGONIST A "BRIDGE CHARACTER"?

Through whose eyes are we seeing a story unfold? Bridge protagonists encounter a place as outsiders—a place that the writer assumes will be new to readers. They convey information; as the bridge character learns, so do the readers. But are they necessary to capture the attention of young readers?

Journalist Nicholas Kristof discussed the realities of the adult attention market in his *New York Times* column after he was criticized for using bridge characters:

> Very often I do go to developing countries where local people are doing extraordinary work, and instead I tend to focus on some foreigner, often some American, who's doing something there. And let me tell you why I do that. The problem that I face—my challenge as a writer—in trying to get readers to care about something like Eastern Congo, is that frankly, the moment a reader sees that I'm writing about Central Africa, for an awful lot of them, that's the moment to turn the page. It's very hard to get people to care about distant crises like that.
>
> One way of getting people to read at least a few [paragraphs] in is to have some kind of a foreign protagonist, some American who they can identify with

as a bridge character. And so if this is a way I can get people to care about foreign countries, to read about them, ideally, to get a little bit more involved, then I plead guilty.

While Kristof might have a point about adult readers, I've come to see that children don't need help identifying with any kind of protagonist, whether near or far. As with language learning, it's far easier for a young person to acquire fluency in imagining other lives than it is for adults. Children see themselves reflected in a protagonist when adults might label that same main character as a "foreigner."

If a story for children features a bridge character who originates outside the setting, ask why the author made that choice. The use of this literary mechanism isn't always problematic. Fantasy and science fiction storytellers, for example, use bridge characters to share details about a magical realm. Often main characters in those genres are actually insiders who don't know much yet about their native identities. As Luke Skywalker learns about the Force, and Harry Potter discovers the world of wizardry, so do we.

Some authors, setting a story in contexts foreign to them, tell it from the perspective of bridge characters to avoid cultural appropriation. Thanks to lived experience and diligent research, this might result in a good story. However, with limited demand in North American and European markets for novels about nonwhite cultures, which books set in Africa, the Middle East, Asia, or Latin America should we consume? When investing time and money, which stories will we read about marginalized contexts that are "foreign" to us within Europe or North America? We may want to prioritize books by people originating in those cultures or subcultures featuring main characters who also originate there instead of bridge characters from the outside. Thankfully, librarians, educators, booksellers, and trusted readers can help us discover such excellent novels.

6. WHO HAS THE POWER?

A storyteller is responsible for assessing privilege because shaping a narrative is an act of power. At the initial stages of conceptualizing a main character, I try to measure how much more powerful I am than my protagonist. If she were to meet me in real life, would she feel at home? How easy would it be for her to entrust me with her secrets? I consider if the combination of all differences between us—in class, age, race, education, gender, and other markers—makes the power gap between us too wide to bridge. If so, her story is better told by someone else.

As a discerning reader, ask who can incite or complete the main character's transformation? Who can effect change and who is given room to be changed? Check for "outside saviors"—a clichéd figure from a more powerful setting who arrives to rescue a marginalized character—and keep an eye out for the tropes we discussed earlier.

7. HOW IS A HISTORY OF OPPRESSION PORTRAYED?

My personal and familial history, especially when it comes to exploitation, war, trauma, slavery, genocide, and other kinds of suffering, will affect both how I read and how I tell a story. What did I gain or lose because of past events that shape this book? Did my ancestors prosper or suffer in the systems and structures portrayed?

Without this sort of historical self-reflection about our own advantaged position, we may not notice that a clothed, up-on-two-legs Babar returns from France to rule four-legged naked beasts that run after the stylish coupe he is driving. We may not see brown-skinned people described as 100 percent cruel (*The Voyage of the Dawn Treader*), French-speaking people depicted as uneducated tropes (*Anne of Green Gables*), or diamond mines in India designed for the prosperity of the protagonist (*A Little Princess*). Understanding how we have benefited from the past can enhance our ability to discern bias in the "bones" of a story.

8. HOW IS THE STORY AUTHENTIC?

How does the author share identities with the protagonist? The word *authentic* and others akin to it are used these days in reviews, in editorial content, and in marketing materials to highlight when authors are writing from a lived experience of marginalization.

Many of us are grateful to the reformers pushing for this accountability; they are changing the market in significant ways. Who tells a story matters, and for too long, powerful voices have commandeered stories about people with less power. A simplistic use of the words *authentic*, *diverse*, or *own voices* to endorse books, however, occludes three facts.

First, to write any work of fiction, an author must cross *some* border of identity—such as age, class, religion, gender, race, culture, class, or education—unless the story is a memoir, in which case it isn't fiction at all.

Second, writers, readers, and characters are at an *intersection* of identities. Which ones between us and the main character must match to gain this generation of gatekeepers' seal of approval? Is it race alone? Or race and class? Or race, class, and gender, and so on?

And third, just because an author and protagonist *do* share an identity doesn't mean that racial and cultural stereotypes won't turn up in a story. The missteps may be fewer. But all storytellers—even those who share the same race as the main character—still must do the hard work that we talked about earlier. Every story, no matter who tells it, must draw upon the exercise of empathetic imagination, honest self-reflection, and diligent research.

When I wrote *Rickshaw Girl*, for example, which is set in Bangladesh, reviewers lauded the fact that I was drawing on my "cultural roots" to tell the story. My main character Naima and I do share an ethnicity and a mother tongue: we are both Bengali. Apart from that, though, she is the daughter of a poor, Muslim rickshaw puller, while my educated, land-owning Hindu ancestors exploited people like her father. Given that country's context and history, Naima and I are about as different as a rich, white suburbanite is from a Black child living in an urban neighborhood. So why do I get a free pass when it comes to "authenticity"? A Muslim non-Bengali storyteller would have told Naima's story in a different way. Would her rendition have been deemed less authentic because she didn't speak the same language as the main character? And how might Naima's story have been more or less suited to be categorized as an "authentic" story were it told by someone who was neither Bengali nor Muslim but instead grew up in poverty?

Questions like these led to my delight when the story was adapted for the screen by a Muslim Bangladeshi director with Muslim Bangladeshi writers and actors. I was thrilled that they would find enough resonance in the novel to want to invest their time and talents to turn it into a movie. And I knew that the lived experience of Muslim Bangladeshi filmmakers would add layers of authenticity as they changed the story significantly. Best of all, I like to imagine that friendships emerging from working on this story are healing grievous rifts formed in the past.

FIND FLAWS AND SEEK VIRTUES

In the United States, we wrestle with the consequences of a history of genocide, slavery, and other atrocities. Descendants of oppressed, exploited, and violated people suffer the consequences of that history, and the continued presence of bias permeates our society. As we try to move forward in healing, laws matter, but so do stories. One of Plato's contemporaries, Damon of Athens, said, "Let me write the songs of a nation, and I care not who writes its laws." That's why consumers and creators of stories for children must think critically about race, culture, and power and put our voices, votes, and dollars to use on behalf of marginalized children.

As we pay attention to flaws and errors in books for children, however, we also want to develop the habit of seeing goodness in them. In reading both classic and contemporary books, we can be on a hunt for virtue as well as bias. How does this story illustrate justice, temperance, prudence, courage, faith, hope, or love? Most good novels—ones we might choose to reread—illuminate at least one or more of the seven virtues we have explored.

Maybe you'll decide that a book isn't virtuous at all; maybe together with the children you love, you will decry it as evil or denounce it as a complete waste of time. That's the beauty of a story: once written and released by the author, readers are free to devour it, drag themselves through it, or toss the entire book away in disgust.

But if we're blessed to find a few books that we read again and again—stories full of virtue in which we steep our souls—it's a worthwhile practice to reflect unflinchingly on their flaws as well. And just as we're called to do with our elders in real life, we might want to try and forgive the authors who penned them. That's what we'll do in the conclusion of this book.

REFLECT AND DISCUSS

1. Choose a novel you've read recently and submit it to the questions in this chapter. Do you notice anything new?

2. Do some research on the author. How do the identities of the author intersect with the identities of the main character? In your view, does that make a difference in the telling of the story?

3. Who was the "other" in your family of origin? What kinds of people, if any, were you warned to avoid?

4. Who is the "other" in your life now? If you can't think of an answer, this assessment is probably unconscious, which might be even more dangerous. Discover it by honestly imagining the prototype of a person you'd want to avoid if possible. Ask for forgiveness and help in overcoming this deep bias.

5. Do you have any friendships with a person in these groups of "others"? Why might it be important to seek some?

6. Go on a hunt for virtue in a book you are reading. How does it shine a light on courage, prudence, temperance, justice, faith, hope, or love?

CONCLUSION

DRINKING TEA WITH THE DEAD

One of the spiritual tasks of maturity is to forgive our parents and grandparents. Jesus challenged his followers to do this work: "Why do you look at the speck of sawdust in your brother's eye and pay no attention to the plank in your own eye? How can you say to your brother, 'Let me take the speck out of your eye,' when all the time there is a plank in your own eye? You hypocrite, first take the plank out of your own eye, and then you will see clearly to remove the speck from your brother's eye" (Matthew 7:3–5). Becoming an adult demands yanking the log out of the soul's eyeballs and having the courage to take a clear-eyed look at the people who raised us. We may have loved them deeply and miss them if they're gone, but oh, how specked were their eyes!

For many of us, the process goes like this: We take stock of hurts our elders inflicted; we don't minimize them. Bringing that pain into the light, we receive healing. Soon, we find ourselves asking for grace to forgive. And then, like Heidi's grandfather, we beg forgiveness for the pain *we* have caused. Here is the real "circle of life," because in time, our descendants must do the same with us.

This necessary work of forgiving those who formed us is challenging, but maturity comes with a capacity to see nuance. Like people from our own past, stories written long ago are not "all good" or "all bad" but a mix of both. If we can accept this, we're invited to revisit classic books periodically, as we do with elderly relatives who love us. We take our tea to the front porch, where a dead author is waiting in a rocking chair. We listen to that auntie's or uncle's story again. Now we can see how their eras shaped them, how they were biased and mistaken, but also that their wisdom might help us resist our own era's crushing and molding of the soul.

I wrote some of this book during three retreats in the town of Carmel-by-the-Sea, California, where some friends graciously offered the use of their place. I'm here now. Janet's grandmother decorated this cozy ranch home, and her grandchildren and great-grandchildren have preserved many of the antiques and books Mrs. Ellis loved, including some of the titles we've discussed in this book. Surrounded by old things, I've been revisiting the stories that accompanied so much of my childhood. I've accepted W. H. Auden's challenge to "break bread with the dead"—that is, to converse with the work of those who have gone before—and come to see that this means forgiving them as well. In the process, I've made peace both with my complicated literary "aunties" and "uncles" and with the flawed stories they created.

This might come a bit easier for those of us originating in cultures that require us to stay in relationship with our elders. When I became a follower of Jesus, one of the first people I had to tell was my maternal grandfather in India. Dadu was a beloved patriarch, and all eleven of his grandchildren still revere him to this day. He was a professor of chemistry during the British Raj, was fluent in several languages, cared for his wife dutifully for years after she was debilitated by a stroke, and raised five children who looked up to him (all five are eighty-something at the time of this writing). Simply put, he was a good man. I wanted his blessing for this spiritual turn of events, but I knew this was unlikely, as our family had been Hindu for generations. Still, I gathered my courage to tell him the truth.

The two of us were on the round veranda overlooking the garden he loved, dipping biscuits into tea. It was monsoon season, so the air was fresh, and a light rain was falling. Crows hidden in the coconut trees complained about the weather, but otherwise, the neighborhood was in silent afternoon-nap mode.

"I've taken Jesus as my guru," I blurted out suddenly. To me, the declaration sounded as harsh as the cawing above our heads.

Dadu never answered quickly. This time, however, his eyes lit up and he responded without hesitation: "Oh, that is superb!"

"Really?" I asked, astonished. "You think so?"

"Most definitely. I won an essay contest as a young man, and the prize was a marvelous book. *The Imitation of Christ*, it was called, a slim volume by a man named Thomas à Kempis. I was sad when I lost my copy during Partition. We fled in such a hurry."

Now there's a plot twist, I remember thinking. "Did you read it, Dadu?"

"Oh, yes. Time and time again. In fact, I memorized passages that still shape me to this day. So you see, in a sense, I, too, consider Jesus my guru."

When I returned home, I sent *The Imitation of Christ* to my grandfather (he wanted the English version that he had received as a young man), and he read it regularly until he died. He was a man who always longed for more virtue, as expressed in letters written until he was in his late nineties.

This pursuit of a life marked by love, faith, hope, temperance, courage, justice, and prudence is beset by failures within and pressure without. Despair, alienation, and favoritism embedded in our era relentlessly try to shape us, aided and abetted by our own self-indulgence, pusillanimity, rashness, rigidity, and other vices. We can take heart from Thomas à Kempis, who wrote, "For it is the grace of Christ, and not our own virtue, that gives us the power to overcome the flesh and the world."

We are strengthened by reading and rereading books written for young readers, which are particularly powerful in forming the soul in addition to the mind. I believe Dadu would have enjoyed reading *Heidi*, *Little Women*, *The Silver Chair*, *The Hobbit*, *A Little Princess*, *Emily of Deep Valley*, and *Anne of Green Gables*. I wish he were here to join our conversation. But I'm glad for your company, dear readers, as we considered these timeless novels. Writing this book has invited me to forgive the dead and once again be taught by them. I hope you have been able to do the same and that your soul, perhaps as tired as mine, has been refreshed.

THE END

Acknowledgments

My parents sacrificed greatly to bring their three daughters to this country. They empowered us to pursue an excellent education and sustained us with superb meals, laughter, tears, visits to the library, music, and storytelling. Meanwhile, my sisters and I learned to keep one another's secrets as we code switched between our traditional Bengali home and North American suburbia. Thank you, family of origin.

Laura Rennert, my literary agent, has guided my career in writing for young people for more than two decades. A book of nonfiction for adult readers is a new venture for me, but Laura is always encouraging when I decide to take a risk. Editor Valerie Weaver-Zercher skillfully shaped this book from conception to conclusion. My gratitude goes to her and to the publicity, marketing, production, sales, design, and editorial teams at Broadleaf Books.

I'm indebted to many people in my church communities, including our sons, James and Timothy, from whom I've received God's love as well as vocational encouragement. The

Perez family loaned me their Carmel cottage to pray, write, and think deeply. My "philosopher-in-a-pocket," Marshall Bierson, reawakened my interest in the virtues through his essay "And All Shall Be Changed: Virtue in the New Creation," which won the Marc Sanders Prize in Philosophy of Religion.

Last but not least, if there's any sound theology in this book, credit goes to twenty-five years' worth of Sunday sermons preached by my husband, the Reverend Doctor Robert K. Perkins. All heresies and errors are due to my shoddy listening skills and lack of virtue. Even so, like you, I remain beloved.

NOTES

INTRODUCTION

3   **"They can break down borders"**: Hazel Rochman, "Against Borders," *Horn Book Magazine*, May 7, 1995, https://tinyurl.com/y24548zf.

3   **"Think of children's books"**: Katherine Rundell, "Story Time: The Five Children's Books Every Adult Should Read," *Guardian*, July 26, 2019, https://tinyurl.com/y2euec4d.

4   **"There are good books"**: W. H. Auden, *Forewords and Afterwords* (New York: Random House, 1973), 291.

5   **"Is there any call"**: J. R. R. Tolkien, lecture adapted into an essay, then retitled "On Fairy-Stories" and included in the appendix to *Tales from the Perilous Realm* (New York: HarperCollins, 2002), 57–58.

5   **"Critics who treat"**: C. S. Lewis, "On Three Ways of Writing for Children," Catholic Culture, accessed December 29, 2020, https://tinyurl.com/y6yq8sxj.

6   **"No book is genuinely free"**: George Orwell, "Why I Write," in *Politics and the English Language and Other Essays*, 1946, https://tinyurl.com/yajr89wn.

6   **"The essential function"**: D. H. Lawrence, "Whitman," in *Studies in Classic American Literature*, ed. Ezra Greenspan and Lindeth Vasey (Cambridge: Cambridge University Press, 2003), 2:148–61.

6   **"moral pap"**: Louisa May Alcott, *Louisa May Alcott: Her Life, Letters, and Journals*, ed. Ednah Cheney (New York: Little, Brown, 1898), 294, https://tinyurl.com/y47cb3g3.

6   **"written to be read"**: Alex Preston, "Why You Should Read Children's Books, Even Though You Are So Old and Wise by Katherine Rundell—Review," *Guardian*, August 5, 2019, https://tinyurl.com/y4987j27.

7   **"I'm not arguing"**: Charlotte Eyre, "Katherine Rundell | 'I Will Be Writing Children's Books until I Am Old,'" Bookseller, March 25, 2019, https://tinyurl.com/y3vkam77.

8   **"[Rundell's] argument"**: Jo Hemmings, "Child's Play: Why You Should Read Children's Books, Even Though You Are So Old and Wise by Katherine Rundell," Lucy Writers, April 5, 2020, https://tinyurl.com/yxz3m5fp.

8   **"Where the children's story"**: C. S. Lewis, *Of Other Worlds: Essays and Stories* (New York: Harcourt, 2002), 24.

8   **"A classic is a book"**: Italo Calvino, *The Uses of Literature* (New York: Houghton Mifflin Harcourt, 1987), 128.

8   **"The great thing"**: Susan Heller Anderson and David W. Dunlap, "New York Day by Day: Author to Readers," *New York Times*, April 25, 1985, https://tinyurl.com/yxfqkrr5.

9   **"Love has its speed"**: Kosuke Koyama, *Three Mile an Hour God* (New York: Orbis, 1980), 7.

9   **"The Web provides"**: Nicholas Carr, *The Shallows: What the Internet Is Doing to Our Brains* (New York: Norton, 2020), 192.

11   **"And fourth"**: *Catechism of the Catholic Church*, part 3 ("Life in Christ"), sec. 1 ("Man's Vocation: Life in the Spirit"), chap. 1 ("The Dignity of the Human Person"), art. 7 ("The Virtues"), https://tinyurl.com/y4fa7adt.

CHAPTER 1

16   **"The book depicts"**: Jean de Brunhoff, *Babar the Elephant* (Paris: Edition du Jardins des Modes, 1931); Adam Gopnik, "Freeing the Elephants: What Babar Brought," *New Yorker*, September 15, 2008, https://tinyurl.com/ycl5n2v9.

16   **"Tintin becomes a hero"**: Hergé, *Tintin in the Congo* (Paris: Éditions de Petit Vingtième, 1931).

17   **"In October 2007"**: Alison Leigh Cowan, "A Library's Approach to Books That Offend," *New York Times*, August 19, 2009, https://tinyurl.com/y2u4sjkh.

17   **"The debate over these books"**: Niraj Chokshi, "Prestigious Laura Ingalls Wilder Award Renamed over Racial Insensitivity," *New York Times*, June 26, 2018, https://tinyurl.com/yb468gbr.

18   **"a black boy"**: J. K. Rowling, *Harry Potter and the Sorcerer's Stone* (New York: Scholastic, 1997), 122.

18   **"a tall black girl"**: J. K. Rowling, *Harry Potter and the Goblet of Fire* (New York: Scholastic, 2000), 261.

18   **"tall black wizard"**: J. K. Rowling, *Harry Potter and the Order of the Phoenix* (New York: Scholastic, 2003), 49.

18   **"tall black boy"**: J. K. Rowling, *Harry Potter and the Half-Blood Prince* (New York: Scholastic, 2005), 143.

19   **"This is despite"**: Hugh Lofting, "Chapter 11: The Black Prince," in *The Story of Doctor Dolittle*, Lit2Go ed., 1920, accessed December 29, 2020, https://tinyurl.com/y6kznlww.

20   **"Today, for example"**: Benedicte Page, "New Huckleberry Finn Edition Censors 'N-Word,'" *Guardian*, January 5, 2011, https://tinyurl.com/y84u7p5k.

22   **"Michael is waiting"**: Mitali Perkins, *The Sunita Experiment* (New York: Little, Brown, 1993).

24   **"The single story":** Chimamanda Adichie, "The Danger of a Single Story," TED talk, 2009, https://tinyurl.com/tglqhre.

26   **"The world of children's literature":** Pooja Makhijani, "What a Forgotten Kids Book Reveals about U.S. Publishing," *Atlantic*, October 3, 2017, https://tinyurl.com/y9dmndyu.

26   **"stories as mirrors":** Rudine Sims Bishop, "Mirrors, Windows, and Sliding Glass Doors," Perspectives, 6, no. 3 (Summer 1990): 9–11.

CHAPTER 2

32   **"Some believe the era":** This transition was discussed by the sociologists Jean-François Lyotard and Jean Baudrillard, who named the era that came next "postmodernity."

36   **"Sometimes we need":** Tori Latham, "The Books Briefing: Poetry of the Past, in the Present," *Atlantic*, August 28, 2020, https://tinyurl.com/y655p8eh.

36   **"When we open":** Alan Jacobs, *Breaking Bread with the Dead: A Reader's Guide to a More Tranquil Mind* (New York: Penguin, 2020).

36   **"art is our chief means":** W. H. Auden, "Some Reflections on the Arts," in *The Complete Works of W. H. Auden*, vol. 6, *1969–1973* (Princeton, NJ: Princeton University Press, 2015), 644.

39   **"The line separating":** Aleksandr Solzhenitsyn, *The Gulag Archipelago, 1918–1956*, vol. 1 (Paris: Éditions du Seuil, 1973).

40   **"Human virtues":** *Catechism of the Catholic Church*, part 3 ("Life in Christ"), sec. 1 ("Man's Vocation: Life in the Spirit"), chap. 1 ("The Dignity of the Human Person"), art. 7 ("The Virtues"), https://tinyurl.com/y2udg2n2.

CHAPTER 3

47   **"Anne is popular"**: Robin Levinson-King, "Anne of Green Gables: The Most Popular Redhead in Japan," BBC News, May 8, 2017, https://www.bbc.com/news/world-us-canada-39809999.

47   **"Anne Shirley provides"**: Levinson-King.

47   **"next door"**: All quotes from *Anne of Green Gables* in this chapter are from the Bantam Classics edition, published in June 1987 by arrangement with Farrar, Straus & Giroux.

49   **"bones of the book"**: This phrase is derived from the author Katherine Paterson's official website, FAQ section, accessed January 9, 2021, http://katherinepaterson.com/faq/.

51   **"savage nations"**: Irene Gammel, *Looking for Anne of Green Gables: The Story of L. M. Montgomery and Her Literary Classic* (New York: St. Martin's Press, 2009), 130.

51   **"Even today North Rustico"**: Gammel, 131.

52   **"My position is too awful"**: Mary Beth Cavert, "Perspectives on the Circumstances of L. M. Montgomery's Death: Was It Suicide or an Accident?," L. M. Montgomery Literary Society, 2014, https://tinyurl.com/y3gt9k83.

54   **"in a few poignant sentences"**: L. M. Montgomery, *Anne of Windy Poplars*, 1936, Project Gutenberg of Australia, chap. 5, http://gutenberg.net.au/ebooks01/0100251h.html.

54   **"Behind an attitude"**: From a homily at morning Mass in the Casa Santa Marta by Pope Francis, "Pope: 'God Calls Us to Be Merciful and Good, Not Rigid,'" *Vatican Radio*, October 24, 2016, https://tinyurl.com/y68nmker.

55   **"Temperance is love"**: De moribus eccl., chap. xv.

58   **"piety, loyalty, duty"**: *Online Etymology Dictionary*, s.v. "pity," accessed December 29, 2020, https://www.etymonline.com/word/pity.

59   **"God conceived as"**: *Merriam-Webster*, s.v. "providence," accessed December 29, 2020, https://tinyurl.com/y3t6zwfh.

62   **"capable of being wounded"**: Brené Brown, *Daring Greatly: How the Courage to Be Vulnerable Transforms the Way We Live, Love, Parent, and Lead* (New York: Avery, 2012), 39.

62   **"Whenever you find tears"**: Frederick Buechner, *Whistling in the Dark: A Doubter's Dictionary* (New York: HarperCollins, 1993), 117.

CHAPTER 4

67   **"It was originally published"**: In German, the titles are *Heidis Lehr- und Wanderjahre* and *Heidi kann brauchen, was es gelernt hat.*

68   **"When Heidi came into my hands"**: Deepa Agarwal, "Great Storytellers for Kids: Johanna Spyri, Beloved Daughter of the Alps," *Indian Express*, January 22, 2020, https://tinyurl.com/y2d5guk2.

69   **"A sense of belongingness"**: R. F. Baumeister and M. R. Leary, "The Need to Belong: Desire for Interpersonal Attachments as a Fundamental Human Motivation," *Psychological Bulletin* 117, no. 3 (1995): 497–529.

69   **"Researchers now identify"**: Ellen E. Lee et al., "High Prevalence and Adverse Health Effects of Loneliness in Community-Dwelling Adults across the Lifespan: Role of Wisdom as a Protective Factor," *International Psychogeriatrics* 31, no. 10 (October 2019): 1447–62, https://tinyurl.com/y9y8n2qs.

70   **"Not everyone"**: For statistics and sources in this paragraph, see Don Berwick, Julianne Holt-Lunstad, and Robin Carusom, "The Health Impact of Loneliness: Emerging Evidence and Interventions," presentation at the National Institute for Health Care Management Foundation, October 15, 2018, https://tinyurl.com/yav53r5f; Sumathi Reddy, "The Mystery around Middle-Age

Suicides," *Wall Street Journal*, June 14, 2018, https://tinyurl.com/yxc4k2lt; Ed Butler, "Why Some Japanese Pensioners Want to Go to Jail," BBC News, January 31, 2019, https://www.bbc.com/news/stories-47033704; and Matthew Bremner, "The Lonely End," *Slate*, June 26, 2015, https://tinyurl.com/y5qu69h8.

71 **"A study by the health company":** "Loneliness and the Workplace," Cigna, 2020, https://tinyurl.com/rpbd6l7.

71 **"Those who use social media":** Brian A. Primack et al., "Social Media Use and Perceived Social Isolation among Young Adults in the U.S.," *American Journal of Preventive Medicine* 53, no. 1 (July 1, 2017): 1–8, https://tinyurl.com/y657mhuh.

73 **"When people are chronically":** Annie Vainshtein, "An Expert Explains Why You Feel So Lonely All the Time," Vice, September 2, 2016, https://tinyurl.com/y5jbgg8d.

73 **"The word longing":** Frederick Buechner, *The Longing for Home: Recollections and Reflections* (San Francisco: HarperSanFrancisco, 1996), 19.

75 **"Embittered by this treatment":** Quotations from *Heidi* come from the gift edition, translated by Elisabeth Stork, published in 1919 by J. B. Lippincott, available online through the Gutenberg library, https://tinyurl.com/y2b7h568.

80 **"She learns more":** English translations of *Heidi* choose different hymns and poetry to replace the author's original choices for the grandmother's "old prayer-book with beautiful songs," but in the German, Spyri was specific in her choices. Hymns read or recited by Heidi include "Die güldne Sonne Voll Freud und Wonne," "Kreuz und Elende," and "Befiehl Du Deine Wege" by Paul Gerhardt and "Gott will's machen, dass die Sachen" by Johann Daniel Herrnschmidt, all written in the seventeenth or eighteenth centuries.

83 **"In confession":** Dietrich Bonhoeffer, *Life Together: The Classic Exploration of Christian Community* (New York: Harper & Row, 1954), 112.

85 **"each of us is more":** Bryan Stevenson, *Just Mercy*, trade paperback ed. (New York: Spiegel & Grau, 2015), 219.

85 **"Like a better version":** Timothy Keller, *The Prodigal God: Recovering the Heart of Christian Faith* (New York: Dutton, 2008).

CHAPTER 5

89 **"No. He's eighty-one":** Quotes from *Emily of Deep Valley* come from the HarperPerennial Modern Classics edition, published in 2010. This chapter echoes and elaborates on some of what I wrote in a foreword to that edition.

89 **"According to a recent":** Kim Parker, Rich Morin, and Julian Menasce Horowitz, "America in 2050," Pew Research Center, March 2019, https://tinyurl.com/y5exzy6c.

90 **"Rates of depression":** Jean M. Twenge et al., "Age, Period, and Cohort Trends in Mood Disorder Indicators and Suicide-Related Outcomes in a Nationally Representative Dataset, 2005–2017," *Journal of Abnormal Psychology* 128, no. 3 (March 14, 2019): 185–99, https://tinyurl.com/y7hgd7s8.

90 **"For all their power":** Jean M. Twenge, "Have Smartphones Destroyed a Generation?," *Atlantic*, September 2017, https://tinyurl.com/y3kxdn4q.

93 **"a broken-winged bird":** Langston Hughes, "Dreams," in *The Collected Poems of Langston Hughes*, ed. Arnold Rampersand (New York: Alfred A. Knopf / Vintage, 1994), https://poets.org/poem/dreams.

93 **"Living without hope":** Jürgen Moltmann, *Theology of Hope* (Minneapolis: Fortress Press, 1993), 33.

94 **"If you are"**: Robert Leahy, "How to Overcome Your Feelings of Hopelessness," Oprah.com, August 5, 2010, https://tinyurl.com/y4pderne.

94 **"Hope is the thing"**: Emily Dickinson, "'Hope' Is the Thing with Feathers," Wikisource, accessed December 29, 2020, https://tinyurl.com/y3kz6u2l.

95 **"As the marsh-hen"**: Sidney Lanier, "The Marshes of Glynn," in *Hymns of the Marshes* (New York: Charles Scribner's Sons, 1907), 45, https://tinyurl.com/y4wbewz9.

96 **"How good is man's life"**: Robert Browning, "David Singing before Saul," in *Men and Women* (Boston: Ticknor & Fields, 1855), https://tinyurl.com/yxageu99.

99 **"From 1899 to 1919"**: Jia Tolentino, "The Little Syria of Deep Valley," *New Yorker*, February 16, 2017, https://tinyurl.com/yyy6556w.

CHAPTER 6

110 **"squat, broad, flat-nosed"**: Christopher Tolkien and Humphrey Carpenter, letter #210, *The Letters of J. R. R. Tolkien* (New York: Houghton Mifflin Harcourt, 1981), 274.

110 **"In *The Return of the King*"**: Christina Warmbrunn, "Dear Tolkien Fans: Black People Exist," *Public Medievalist*, September 24, 2020, https://tinyurl.com/yy2lgclf.

111 **"I didn't intend it"**: Transcript by Peter Collier of a recording of the original 1964 interview taken by Denys Geroult and broadcast in 1971 on the BBC Radio 4 program "Now Read On," available on YouTube, https://tinyurl.com/y3m7tyce.

111 **"Thank you for your letter"**: Tolkien and Carpenter, letter #30, 37.

112 **"Another regret he had"**: Tolkien and Carpenter, letter #61, 73.

112 **"never minded explaining"**: J. R. R. Tolkien, *The Hobbit*, authorized paperback ed., published by arrangement with Houghton Mifflin, First Ballantine Books rev. ed. (New York: Random House, 1982), 95.

112 **"Merry he could be"**: J. R. R. Tolkien, *Unfinished Tales: The Lost Lore of Middle-Earth* (New York: Del Rey, 1988), 406.

113 **"stretching forth"**: Thomas Aquinas, *Summa Theologiae*, second part of the second part, question 129, 1485. https://www.newadvent.org/summa/3129.htm, accessed January 25, 2021.

113 **"In his book *The Hero*"**: Joseph Campbell, *The Hero with a Thousand Faces* (New York: Pantheon, 1949).

115 **"the ability to do something"**: *Oxford Dictionary*, s.v. "courage," accessed December 29, 2020, https://www.lexico.com/en/definition/courage.

115 **"I learned that courage"**: Nelson Mandela, *Long Walk to Freedom: The Autobiography of Nelson Mandela* (New York: Little, Brown, 1994), 622.

118 **"Off you go"**: Tolkien, *Hobbit*, 29.

118 **"Sometimes the bravest"**: Brown, *Daring Greatly*, 243.

123 **"the moment when each"**: John Yorke, *Into the Woods: A Five Act Journey into Story* (New York: Penguin, 2013).

125 **"They think, 'It's dangerous'"**: Cindy Wooden, "There but for the Grace of God: What Pope Francis Thinks of Prisoners," *National Catholic Register*, May 28, 2015, https://tinyurl.com/y5b9xx9m.

125 **"Riddles were"**: Tolkien, *Hobbit*, 73–75.

127 **"There is more in you"**: Tolkien, 290.

128 **"Life shrinks or expands"**: Anaïs Nin, *The Diary of Anaïs Nin*, vol. 3, *1939–1944* (New York: Harcourt Brace Jovanovich, 1969), 125.

CHAPTER 7

132 **"as close as a sister"**: Joan Acocella, "Ladies Choice," *New Yorker*, August 27, 2018, https://tinyurl.com/yyyvbo9b.

135 **"This virtue, he wrote"**: Thomas Aquinas, *Summa Theologiae*, second part of the second part, question 141, 1485. https://www.newadvent.org/summa/3141.htm, accessed January 25, 2021.

136 **"never enough"**: Brown, *Daring Greatly*, 27.

136 **"[I] helped start"**: Alcott, *Louisa May Alcott*, 344.

137 **"I should like"**: All quotes from *Little Women* in this chapter are from Dilithium Press, Children's Classics edition, published in 1987, distributed by Crown.

138 **"Berkeley researchers"**: Joshua Brown and Joel Young, "How Gratitude Changes You and Your Brain," *Greater Good Magazine*, June 6, 2017, https://tinyurl.com/y43ah5ls.

138 **"Thanks to a tempering"**: Interestingly, if adaptations reflect the mores of the filmmaker's time, Meg's celebration of her vocation as wife and mother is portrayed wholeheartedly by actor Emma Watson in Greta Gerwig's 2019 version of *Little Women*. "What was really important to me about playing Meg is that I think her desire to be a mother and a wife is a feminist choice," Watson said in an interview. "There's this idea that in order to be a feminist you need to reject marriage. But a union with a spouse is what Meg wants most in her heart. As she says to Jo on her wedding day: just because my dreams are not the same as yours does not make them unimportant." From "Emma Watson Follows Her Dreams in *Little Women*," POP!, February 13, 2020, https://tinyurl.com/y4sytxfn, accessed January 25, 2021.

CHAPTER 8

150 **"a little figure":** All quotes from *A Little Princess* in this chapter are from the 1963 edition published by J. B. Lippincott.

155 **"By 1914":** "The Lascars: Britain's Colonial Sailors," Our Migration Story, accessed January 9, 2021, https://tinyurl.com/y3nmsjph.

156 **"During the heyday":** Joseph McQuade, "Colonialism Was a Disaster and the Facts Prove It," *The Conversation*, September 26, 2017, https://tinyurl.com/ydxzl6ot.

157 **"a habit whereby man":** Thomas Aquinas, *Summa Theologiae*, second part of the second part, question 58, 1485, accessed January 9, 2021, https://www.newadvent.org/summa/3058.htm.

157 **"Justice is the moral virtue":** *Catechism of the Catholic Church*, part 3 ("Life in Christ"), sec. 1 ("Man's Vocation: Life in the Spirit"), chap. 1 ("The Dignity of the Human Person"), art. 7 ("The Virtues"), para. 1807, https://tinyurl.com/y3v5hmy9, accessed January 25, 2021.

160 **"The 'no matter whatness'":** Gregory Boyle, *Tattoos on the Heart: The Power of Boundless Compassion* (New York: Free Press, 2010), 54.

162 **"A Litany of Humility":** "A Litany of Humility"—written by Merry Cardinal del Val, secretary of state, to Pope Saint Pius X—was added to the *Jesuit Prayer Book* in 1963.

166 **"Aquinas says that anger":** Rebecca Konyndyk DeYoung, *Glittering Vices: A New Look at the Seven Deadly Sins and Their Remedies* (Ada, MI: Brazos Press, 2009), 122.

168 **"Everything can be taken":** Viktor E. Frankl, *Man's Search for Meaning* (Boston: Beacon Press, 2006), 66.

170 **"a 'preferential option'":** From a 2013 apostolic exhortation by Pope Francis, *Evangelii gaudium* [The joy of the Gospel], chap. 4, sec. 2, para. 197, https://tinyurl.com/yxdajll4.

CHAPTER 9

176 **"Author Philip Pullman"**: John Ezard, "Narnia Books Attacked as Racist and Sexist," *Guardian*, June 3, 2002, https://tinyurl.com/y45nepnq.

178 **"And please notice"**: Devin G. Brown, "Are The Chronicles of Narnia Sexist and Racist?," keynote address presented at the 12th Annual Conference of the C. S. Lewis and Inklings Society, Calvin College, March 28, 2009, https://www.lewissociety.org/brown/.

178 **"He might even elaborate"**: Brown.

178 **"After writing them"**: After Joy Davidman's death, C. S. Lewis would write, "She was my daughter and my mother, my pupil and my teacher, my subject and my sovereign; and always, holding all these in solution, my trusty comrade, friend, shipmate, fellow-soldier" in *A Grief Observed* (London: Faber & Faber, 1961), 39.

179 **"We have a strange illusion"**: C. S. Lewis, *The Problem of Pain* (New York: HarperOne, 2015), 54–55.

182 **"Ignatius of Loyola's"**: The Puhl translation of *The Spiritual Exercises* has been used by Jesuits, spiritual directors, retreat leaders, and others since it was first published in 1951. Puhl translated directly from studies based on the autograph, which are the Exercises in Ignatius's own handwriting, https://tinyurl.com/p455vay.

182 **"We also reflect"**: For a simple introduction to the practice, perfect for aficionados of children's literature, read *Sleeping with Bread: Holding What Gives You Life* by Dennis Linn and Sheila Fabricant Linn (Mahwah, NJ: Paulist Press, 1995).

184 **"Ah, there you are"**: C. S. Lewis, *The Silver Chair* (New York: HarperCollins, 1981), 75.

185 **"Remember, remember"**: Lewis, 27.

187 **"It was absolute misery"**: Lewis, 101.

188 **"The children huddled"**: Lewis, 147.

189 **"Aslan raised his head"**: C. S. Lewis, *The Last Battle* (New York: HarperCollins, 1984), 168–69.

191 **"no Narnia"**: Lewis, *Silver Chair*, 180.

191 **"I'm on Aslan's side"**: Lewis, 182.

CHAPTER 10

196 **"I think it was"**: Katherine Paterson's official website, FAQ section, accessed January 9, 2021, http://katherinepaterson.com/faq/.

201 **"A 'new phenomenon'"**: Susan Gonzalez, "Director Spike Lee Slams 'Same Old' Black Stereotypes in Today's Films," *Yale Bulletin and Calendar* 29, no. 21 (March 2, 2001), http://archives.news.yale.edu/v29.n21/story3.html.

202 **"you is smart"**: This is a refrain repeated in the novel *The Help* by Kathryn Stockett (New York: G. P. Putnam's Sons, 2009).

202 **"Throughout the world"**: Leah Donnella, "Is Beauty in the Eyes of the Colonizer?," *Code Switch*, NPR, February 6, 2019, https://tinyurl.com/y3ymg2ue.

203 **"Perhaps the most insidious"**: Huberta Jackson-Lowman, "An Analysis of the Impact of Eurocentric Concepts of Beauty on the Lives of Afrikan American Women," in *Afrikan American Women: Living at the Crossroads of Race, Gender, Class, and Culture*, ed. Huberta Jackson-Lowman (San Diego: Cognella Academic, 2014), 155–72, https://tinyurl.com/yxre3vqj.

204 **"The characters are white"**: Ursula K. Le Guin, "Some Assumptions about Fantasy," speech, BookExpo America, Chicago, June 4, 2004.

204 **"Le Guin won the battle"**: To see both covers, visit Ana Grilo and Thea James, "Cover Matters: On Whitewashing," Book Smugglers, September 26, 2010, https://tinyurl.com/y2nftk6p.

206 **"Very often I do go":** Nicholas Kristof, "Westerners on White Horses," *New York Times*, July 14, 2010, https://tinyurl.com/y3jmwp5e.

211 **"I was thrilled":** See http://rickshawgirlmovie.com for more.

CONCLUSION

219 **"For it is the grace of Christ":** Thomas à Kempis, *Bread and Wine: Readings for Lent and Easter* (Walden, NY: Plough, 2003), 38.